SOCIAL SERVICE
WORKPLACE BULLYING

Also available from Lyceum Books, Inc.

Advisory Editor: Thomas M. Meenaghan, *New York University*

Child Sexual Abuse: Best Practices for Interviewing and Treatment
by Monit Cheung

Best Practices in Community Mental Health: A Pocket Guide
edited by Vikki L. Vandiver

Civic Youth Work: Cocreating Democratic Youth Spaces
edited by Ross VeLure Roholt, Michael Baizerman, and R. W. Hildreth

Social Work with HIV and AIDS: A Case-Based Guide
by Diana Rowan and Contributors

The Recovery Philosophy and Direct Social Work Practice
by Joseph Walsh

Food for Thought: A Two-Year Cooking Guide for Social Work Students
by Kevin Corcoran and Collaborators

Secondary Traumatic Stress and the Child Welfare Professional
by Josephine G. Pryce, Kimberly K. Shackelford, and David H. Pryce

Children and Loss: A Practical Handbook for Professionals
edited by Elizabeth C. Pomeroy and Renée Bradford Garcia

SOCIAL SERVICE WORKPLACE BULLYING
A BETRAYAL OF GOOD INTENTIONS

KATHRYN BROHL
Licensed Marriage and Family Therapist
(LMFT)

LYCEUM
BOOKS, INC.

Chicago, IL 60637

© 2013 by Lyceum Books, Inc.

Published by

LYCEUM BOOKS, INC.
5758 S. Blackstone Ave.
Chicago, Illinois 60637
773+643-1903 (Fax)
773+643-1902 (Phone)
lyceum@lyceumbooks.com
http://www.lyceumbooks.com

7 6 5 4 3 2   14 15 16 17 18

ISBN 978-1-935871-29-3

Cover credit: © Ginasanders | Dreamstime.com.

Printed in the United States of America.

Library of Congress Cataloging-in-Publication Data

Brohl, Kathryn.
   Social service workplace bullying : a betrayal of good intentions / Kathryn Brohl.
      p. cm.
   Includes bibliographical references and index.
   ISBN 978-1-935871-29-3 (pbk. : alk. paper)
   1. Social workers—Professional relationships. 2. Human services personnel—Professional relationships. 3. Social service—Psychological aspects. 4. Social workers—Psychology.
5. Bullying in the workplace. I. Title.
   HV40.35.B766   2013
   361.3068′3—dc23
                                                        2012042575

For Joe, Tristan, Ellie, Susan, and Justin
my favorite posse

Contents

Preface

Writing about bullying in the social service workplace was counterintuitive for me. When I began my career, the topic was as far from my head as becoming a Lawrence Welk groupie. My previous books had addressed different variations of trauma-informed care. It had never occurred to me to write about bad behavior on the part of employees in my line of work toward their coworkers. Yet, for the past several years, bullying in the helping profession has become a problem, and one which continues to fly under the recognition radar. Fortunately, as the overall issue of workplace bullying comes to light, awareness about coworker bullying within the helping profession will continue to grow as well.

I wrote this book because, during my thirty-five years on the job, I've observed a disturbing trend within my profession. It's growing—along with funding cutbacks and data-focused agendas—meaner. By virtue of social service organizations' social structures, bullying has emerged within many of them, and workers find themselves separated from their professional ideals. And this gap is widening.

I've observed leadership lose its perspective, especially when more of the leaders (administrators) now represent vastly different backgrounds. Thirty years ago, a lawyer would not have led a ten million dollar social service organization. Human services have morphed into data-focused, rather than client-focused, entities. This disturbs me. By bowing to national, state, and local legislative whims, and perhaps misplaced organization leadership and focus, my profession has lost its way, and workplace bullying has taken hold.

Like its cousin, domestic violence, social service workplace bullying has been known to blame its victims, at the very least viewing them with suspicion. Familiar remarks such as "If they [the victims] don't like their treatment, why don't they just leave?" or "They should just get over it" reflect unenlightened perceptions. As with abusive partners in the realm of domestic violence, workplace bullies should be required to be reeducated or leave the premises. Bullying is abuse by a perpetrator, but for too long the focus has been more on blaming victims than on dealing with the bullies.

Social service workplace bullying is complex and does not exist in a vacuum. Workers are targeted (bullied) for many reasons by coworkers, who have normally entered the field with the best of intentions. But like a romantic partnership, one's job can either feed or starve a soul. Individuals who assert their power and authority by using inappropriate behaviors need to be recognized and reeducated.

In addition, research has found that helping others—and social services is all about helping others—is a positive form of self-care (see *Scientific American*, July/August 2012). When, however, this form of self-care within the work environment is challenged because employees are unable to do their jobs owing to bullying, the concept of self-care at work becomes distorted.

This book serves as a practical field guide for students working at their practicums, as well as for seasoned social work professionals. For both older and newer students of the helping arts, identifying and addressing on-the-job bullying can divert impending problems and unnecessary worker turnover, alleviating not only huge financial costs but loss of talented workers as well. In addition, this book provides reality checks, and arms professionals to navigate their way through a potential bullying experience.

Social service workplaces must transform their cultures to reflect healthy worker interactions and zero tolerance for workplace bullying. People within our profession are normally passionate about their work, embarking on their careers with the best of intentions. Let's keep their focus going by addressing social service workplace bullying.

I hope you find this book a helpful resource.

—Kathryn Brohl, LMFT

Acknowledgments

Wonderfully competent people shared their management expertise and wisdom. For your leadership insights, thank you to Lee Cockerell, Diane DeMark, Babette Hankey, Patricia O'Gorman, Nancy Dreicer, and Jamie Chesler.

To former Lt. Paula Coughlin, thank you for your courage in standing up to the bullies, and your brave contribution to changing a flawed system.

Thank you to the people who anonymously volunteered their personal bullying experiences, and bravely weathered the storms. I admire you greatly.

To anyone I've unintentionally bullied, please accept my apology. I didn't know any better, but trust me, I've learned.

Thank you to family and friends who supported me on this new journey. My grandchildren, daughter, and son-in-law who keep me laughing. My neighbor, Meg, and my dear sister, Chris, were my reality checks.

And thank you, especially, to my dear husband, Joseph Hege, who was always there to support me, even when I became grumpy.

I would also like to thank my publisher, David Follmer at Lyceum Books, Inc., for recognizing a need for this book. And thanks to Tom Meenaghan, for those helpful comments. I would also like to thank the skilled and extremely knowledgeable guidance and editing from Lyn Rosen, Catherine Dixon, and Siobhan Drummond at Lyceum. They worked, in such a respectful way, to make this a better book.

How Did We Get Here?
Why Social Service Workplace
Bullying Does Not Exist in a Vacuum

For years, my backyard has been my quiet spot for contemplative observation. From my backyard perspective, interaction between the plant and animal world seems almost seamless and magical. And yet, a closer look reveals a never-ending cycle of building and destroying, in spite of weather conditions or other intrusions.

In my backyard, life seeks its own balance as cardinals and squirrels vie for food (under the nose of our cat, making her appointed gatekeeping rounds about the small property). For the most part, my backyard has acquired its own rhythm. Yet its rhythm and synchronicity are fragile and can be disrupted with the appearance of an outside force. This disruption normally occurs on Wednesdays, with the arrival of our "landscapers."

My landscapers are the guys who appear suddenly, carrying shiny, loud, sharp-cutting machines and wearing large noise mufflers and protective headgear that make them look like terrorists. And their appearance does terrify all things living in my backyard; life seems frozen for several minutes after their departure. I wonder what deeper damage is being done because of the invasion, and ponder other ways to tame my bushes and grass without introducing fear into the system.

It's not a stretch of the imagination to liken my backyard and my landscapers to bullying in the workplace. In a work environment, people pretty much want to survive with as little disruption as possible as they balance their work against the backdrop of their overall lives. Part of surviving is working with others to achieve personal and professional goals, as well as giving work some form of meaning or purpose. When bullying or bullies appear through aggressive systems of operation, or otherwise threatening management patterns, people will generally respond to their fear by freezing, withdrawing, or exhibiting aggressive or submissive survival responses.

As with my backyard habitat, the balance of things at work is disrupted when survival is truly, or even just perceived to be, at risk. Bullying in the form of the overpowering aggressiveness of the landscapers' presence terrifies and disrupts the natural peace of my small world. There is an interplay between this unnatural force and the plant and animal world, as there is an interplay between unnatural or negative patterns of social structures and human behavior that create bullying in the workplace. The result is fear, and fear's attendant responses never bring out the best in people.

> **Social Structure**
>
> The way in which society is organized into predictable relationships, patterns of social interaction, or the way in which people respond to each other. These patterns are to some extent independent of the particular individual, and exert a force which shapes behavior and identity (Schaefer & Lamm, 2012).

Workplace Bullying and the Interplay Between Social Structure and Human Behavior

To explain how workplace bullying has evolved within the social services field requires an examination of the interplay between social structures or systems, and human behavior. Social structures can have a positive or negative impact on human behavior. They are major causal factors behind bullying behaviors among coworkers in the field of social services.

Present-day social service workplace bullying has gone virtually unrecognized, and when acknowledged, has been pretty much ignored. Few social structures within social services have recognized it as a problem. But it is a problem, which causes needless suffering and worker turnover at huge psychological and financial cost. Ironically, conventional thinking would presume that if bullying occurs at all, examples are rare. This thinking is false.

Understandably, the notion that social service professionals engage in less than sterling behaviors with one another doesn't make sense to most people. Wrapping our minds around the fact that human services policies, practice, funding, and leadership (social) structures converge to create a perfect storm for mistreating coworkers is bewildering and highlights the reality that bullying within human services can be more complex than in other work environments.

This book was written to support and inform bullied victims, or "targets," as they recognize, address, and give meaning to their bad experiences. I hope that it will help to reeducate bullies as well, informing larger systems that contribute to the problem. It could also be described as a "field guide" for beginning, intermediate, and senior professionals, as it pertains to understanding workplace social structure and other contributors to bullying on the job.

And, while explaining how the workplace bullying problem has evolved into its present incarnation, this book will also describe how to identify, examine the effects of, address, and resolve bullying without necessarily leaving one's job; or, at the very least, departing with one's integrity intact. Bullying leaves terrible scars and causes emotional and physical suffering, further described in Chapter 5. Bullying is a real workplace issue, but victims often blame themselves for the fallout from their experiences.

Preparing for the Future

Graduate students, these days, can look forward to becoming supervisors within two or three years of entering the field. Understanding how real-life workplaces function as reflections of their social structures, in addition to the professional and personal pitfalls that can result from those structures, prepares them to identify and avert possible bullying on the job. Integrating the fact that social structures are mirrored through employee behavior will also help them manage staff with zero tolerance for bullying.

Once upon a time, in the beginning . . . agency founders never intended to create hostile and mean-spirited work environments. Mission statements speak to alleviating human suffering and respecting client rights. Yet, at closer look, these mission statements don't often equally emphasize respecting and supporting staff. Human service organizations exist to help people in need, and can ignore the fact that workplace structures have much to do with the quality of help provided. When social service organizations allow bullying to exist, employee morale plummets and a negative chain of events follows.

Social structures can promote a unique form of workplace bullying that exists in social services and is different from that found in other work environments. For one thing, bullying is just not "supposed to" happen in the social service workplace because of the nature of the work. These different structures/phenomena will be discussed throughout this book.

The contributing phenomena that incubate and promote bullying encompass the following social structures and interplay:

- Management structure (meaning specifically the "vertical" structure of management within social service organizations reflective of the long history of the English Poor Laws superimposed early on in U.S. social welfare),

- Conflicting perceptions of organization missions,

- Isolation and social disengagement through psychological estrangement (alienation),

- Superimposed policies that cause a consistently shifting work environment,

- Funding focus, structures, and constraints,

- Workplace inertia, and

- Communication

Diagram A

This diagram represents the seven contributing social structure phenomena that influence social service workplace bullying.

Vertical Management Structure

Conflicting Mission Perceptions   Psychological Estrangement

Social Service Workplace Bullying

Shifting Policies   Communication

Workplace Inertia   Funding Structures & Constraints

> ### Workplace Bullying
>
> Workplace bullying will be fully defined in Chapter 2, but there is world-wide consensus with experts Gary and Ruth Namie that:
>
> Bullying in the workplace is repeated use of aggressive or unreasonable, subtle or overt, behavior, which can include verbal attacks, threatening gestures, psychological behaviors, and abusive attitudes toward coworkers.

A Closer Look at Contributing Phenomena
Vertical Organization Structures

Social service organizations frequently maintain a vertically (up and down) structured management system of operation, rather than a horizontal or more transparent organizational structure. Vertically structured organizations are known for inhibiting a natural flow of communication to the right people for several reasons.

> Organization structure is defined as, "the way in which organizations arrange people and jobs, so that goals can be met" (Schein, 2010).

Relationships among positions are normally identified by layers of job responsibility, and usually illustrated as a pyramid, with a few leaders at the top who make the key decisions. The group of decision makers becomes broader as it descends the pyramid. Decisions and strategies must pass through several supervisors and managers, in contrast to horizontal, or flat, organization structures, which have fewer layers between administrators and frontline staff.

Layers within vertical management organizations are hierarchical. In addition, vertically structured organizations, also known as traditional organization structures, are characterized by distinct job classifications and top-down authority structures.

Mid- to larger-size social welfare systems normally have multiple layers that end at the top personnel, who then report to board members and government entities (where local, state, or federal funding is distributed, when laws or policies regarding operationalizing the organizations are in place).

Vertical organization structures were set in motion hundreds of years ago and date back to the English Poor Law of 1601 (see Chapter 7). The goal of this law was to reduce the costs of poor relief (Mandelker, 1956). A general perception existed that people in need were more or less responsible for their problems. Many of the law's guiding principles continue today, and two that pertain to this conversation include:

1. Identifying who was worthy of receiving help (normally noblemen and clerics made those decisions), and

2. Keeping costs of service to a minimum. People in low positions were needed to do the difficult work within society.

The Poor Law, already embedded within the U.S. social welfare system, merged with the need to begin to organize and structure systems of care in the later part of the nineteenth century, when the industrial revolution was in play. Social service organization structure mirrored German sociologist and engineer Max Weber's conclusions that when societies embrace capitalism, bureaucracy is the inevitable result. It was also his thinking that power is ascribed to positions rather than to individuals holding those positions. The establishment of this form of structure makes sense, given that most social service agencies were, and continue to be, led by prominent community businesspeople serving on their boards.

Also contributing to vertically structured organization was Henri Fayol's ideas of invoking unity within the management chain of command, embracing authority, discipline, task specializations, and other aspects of organizational power and job separation (Fayol, 1916). The perception of "one best way of doing a job" is the traditional and more prominent approach to management in larger organizations (Taylor, 1912).

Within the realm of social service workplace bullying, vertically structured organizations can place individuals in positions they are not prepared to handle, affording them more negative power, particularly when some awarded positions are based on politics rather than job qualification. Most people are probably familiar with lawmakers, government officials, organization administrators, or even program supervisors who, because they lack management education and training, sometimes misuse their power by bullying to attain their goals.

The hierarchical layout and top-down decision making within vertical organizations promotes other bullying contributors, such as inertia, to surface. On the other hand, horizontal, or lateral, organizational structures are less likely to incubate bullying cultures, owing to shared decision making and transparency when workers are involved in problem-solving and planning. These more open systems promote creativity among employees as well, encouraging the natural creative instinct within human beings. (Leadership will be further discussed in Chapter 8.)

Conflicting Perceptions of Organization Mission

As human services professionals move up the chain of command, mission focus can veer off in different directions. For example, a newly hired graduate-level employee begins working at a drug and alcohol rehabilitation center, with the intention of counseling individuals with substance addictions. His older supervisor, who has been working with the same population for fifteen years, has a different perspective than the new worker, regarding their professional goals. While the new employee earnestly commits to radically changing lives, his supervisor feels her professional goals are met when clients can stay sober for more than a week after leaving detox. In this scenario, divergent perspectives could contribute to a bullying experience, if one of these perspectives is held by the majority of workers, who marginalize or "ice out" others with different perspectives.

Mission interpretation and focus has everything to do with leadership and board member input, often tied to funding and social service agendas. This is not a bad thing, but if mission interpretation is not consistently messaged to staff, people begin to veer off into "doing their own thing," prompting erroneous assumptions and communication breakdown.

While ascending the management ladder, workers' professional missions can mutate from what is good for clients, to what is even better for personal careers. If one's goal is power, then looking out for clients and coworkers may take second place, prompting prospective administrators to block communication, to gossip, and/or to take credit for others' work. Their priorities around organization mission lose their focus.

Achieving an administrator position often means establishing new professional goals that have even more to do with politics, and keeping the position. While it's not politically correct to admit, a natural concern for administrators has to do with employees gossiping about them. The need to count on key people within the organization becomes essential. Thus, an inner circle of key, nonthreatening decision makers is identified. As a result, due to the vertical structure of the organization, administrators may not receive honest feedback—particularly when individuals within the inner circle choose to block communication from other employees.

Once atop the pyramid, administrators now report to even higher authorities, who represent government or other funding entities or are board members, that may or may not share the same political views or agendas. Newly elected government officials frequently appoint persons to high-level governing positions that control policies, which can be counterintuitive to sound social service practice and mission. As social service administrators shift gears to accommodate these changing policies, there is a chance they may become emotionally disconnected from their organization's mission as well.

Psychological Estrangement (Alienation)

The term *alienation*, within this context, is used to describe objectively observable states of separateness occurring in human groups. An older usage viewed alienation as a subjective, individual condition (Johnson, 1976). Psychological estrangement or alienation, within the context of workplace bullying, refers to feeling separated from the work environment and work group, owing to many different factors triggered by workplace bullying.

A natural outgrowth of psychological estrangement at work is to emotionally cut one's self off from social aspects of the job, or disconnect from coworkers. As a result, an upper-level administrator may emotionally disconnect from employees, and perhaps the organization. His or her ability to recognize and appreciate staff or address workplace problems can become impaired. For example, an administrator may begin a pattern of isolation, seldom venturing outside the office, and relying on key individuals to bring back information, which, depending on the messenger's intentions, may be exaggerated or inaccurate.

If mid-level managers experience estrangement, they are also less likely to recognize bullying among coworkers. They can become myopic with regard to job tasks, isolate themselves, or engage with only those who share their views, and/or act out with supervisees who question their authority.

When frontline staff experience psychological estrangement, they tend to disengage from coworkers, and run the risk of viewing clients as part of their problem. They may also over-engage with clients, and employ an "us against them" sort of acting out with their supervisors. They may even encourage bullying within the system of care, particularly when they feel they're carrying the torch for the entire social welfare system.

Psychological estrangement desensitizes workers at every tier within the work culture, and erodes the ability to view one's circumstances from an objective perspective, especially when bullying is occurring within the workplace. Feelings of alienation can surface over time when workers are asked to digest and adjust to ever-changing policies, funding cutbacks, staff turnover, chronic client problems, and other ongoing challenges that sap their energy and take the joy out of their work.

More importantly, bullied/targeted workers become psychologically estranged when they have gone unrecognized for their contributions, been erroneously blamed for problems outside of their control, gossiped about, more or less separated from persons in power, and diminished by coworkers.

Shifting Policies

Going back five hundred years, the English Poor Law was guided by another principle, which assumed that change is inevitable because previous efforts, criticized as insufficient, will soon be the subject of reform. Truth be told, change *is* inevitable. Lawmakers, however, continuously play with social service policies, because they, most often, hold the purse strings. Even community organization board members, when they are large donors, play this card.

Consequently, social service organizations are often whipped back and forth between "new and improved" policies and government structures that dictate which way the funding wind will blow. The upshot of these bending and impending policies is that most social service organizations stay in a constant state of high alert in planning for or implementing new guidelines, or adjusting to budget cutbacks.

The general hyperaroused cultural state of affairs trickles down to a social structure within social services that makes bullying possible. Rigid timelines, program cutbacks, people scrambling to keep their jobs, and unclear messaging about change contribute to people inappropriately reacting to pressure by taking their fears and stress out on coworkers through bullying.

Funding Structures and Constraints

Diminishing budgets in tough economies pile on more stress in social service environments. If budget cutbacks continue, at some point the question becomes how does an organization keep its doors open, and at what cost to those in need? Often, it's a matter of deciding to cut evidence-based programs no longer prioritized by lawmakers.

A competition for finite resources creates a hierarchical structure in which the most powerful position has the greatest access to resources and distributes those resources based on a politically motivated discernment of need. This system sustains itself by keeping some positions of authority to itself, and allocating other positions of service to an appointed authority. For example, authority is given to a new provider of service because of the lobbying effort made by that particular provider. But the deciding entity continues to keep its power. These two entities work in a kind of silent "scratch each other's back" modus operandi, leaving other organizations scrambling, and bullied out of the community social service system.

In addition, bullies in positions of power often achieve their status because of their aggressive personalities. These individuals do not always come from human service educational backgrounds, and their focus can be more on operationalizing and streamlining systems through political rather than altruistic methods, in order to meet legislative agendas that may have nothing to do with compassionate care. A natural trickle-down effect can occur where like attitudes and behaviors are integrated throughout the workplace.

Consequently, conflicts may surface as disparate values collide among other staff members with different perceptions about how to provide best practice in social service, inviting bullying into the system of care.

Workplace Inertia

Social service workers with longevity are usually associated with workplace inertia, theoretically because they're more likely to be desensitized to their jobs, and entrenched in not wanting to make more work for themselves. Yet, workplace inertia occurs when groups of people, whether they're new or seasoned, adopt habits that inhibit them from changing. When inertia takes hold, people become less than their capabilities, and bullying can enter the picture.

For example, an older student graduates with a master's degree in social work and is hired at a child welfare organization. She worked in retail fashion for twenty years but wanted to give her life more meaning by entering the field of human services. Her first day on the job, her supervisor advises her not to speak with clients when shadowing her peer mentor. During the shadowing experience, the new worker notices that her peer mentor doesn't spend much time with a client and is vague about getting back to him regarding his court date. Concerned, the new worker seeks out her supervisor and shares her observation. Her supervisor's response sets the stage for potential bullying: "This is how we've always done it. There is no time. Clients get used to it."

When employees are at the job longer, without transitioning to different responsibilities or otherwise learning new tasks, they become greater risks for contributing to workplace inertia. If yearly bonuses and pay increases are attached to their long-standing employment, many may feel threatened by newer employees with an eye toward innovation or a different slant on doing the job. Longtime supervisors/managers, and even more recently hired, lazier workers, can become dangerous bullies when threatened with being unseated at work.

Flawed Communication

When employees seek help for on-the-job bullying, communication weighs heavily in the picture. For example, if an inequality wall exists between a worker and an unresponsive coworker with more influence, communication between the two can become impaired, resulting in a target's needless suffering and psychological estrangement.

In vertically structured work organizations, where communication can be log-jammed because of the multilayered structure, it takes longer to bring bullying issues to the attention of decision makers. When targeted workers want to report their abuse, they may be blocked by their supervisors or supervisees, human resources directors, and upper-level managers who've been given flawed information or no information at all. For example, in one organization, a counselor who was friendly with the COO outside the agency shared incorrect information about her direct supervisor. Without checking the truth, she repeated client exaggerations about their experiences with the supervisor, who had been setting boundaries with those clients. Consequently, the COO took her friend's word as fact, and proceeded to marginalize the supervisor out of her job.

Flawed communication also occurs when coworkers fail to share pertinent information, setting the stage for bad feelings to surface. It occurs when supervisors/managers fail to communicate appreciation, and administrators remain vague about organizational change, or ignore employee concerns.

Ambivalence plays a large role in when, and how, information gets communicated. If one feels ambivalent about another worker, information may flow at a slower pace. In addition, flawed communication through technology supports less face-to-face discussion, where body language and voice inflection can be picked up to clarify communication.

Capturing the Causes Reveals the Complexity of the Problem

Social service workplace bullying is unique compared with bullying at other workplaces. The problem incubates within different embedded sectors of the overall organization, and even beyond. Yet, as awareness about workplace bullying grows, these causal factors will be acknowledged as recognizable, and as specific problems that can be addressed to move forward to create zero tolerance policies for bullying. These underlying contributors remind us that social service workplace bullying is complex, just as human beings are complex.

We all seek to tame our wild and impulsive natures, especially in the workplace. Yet it should not be at the cost of deadening worker creativity and fulfillment. It is a fine balance.

2

Social Service Workplace Bullying: A Curious Irony

Food chain—"A sequence of organisms in a community in which each member feeds on the one below it." (*Webster's New World College Dictionary*, 1999)

Tag—You're It!

Austen stood outside his supervisor's door, breathing deeply, anticipating his boss's barrage of put-downs and humiliations. Austen's two-month-old client had just died from Sudden Infant Death Syndrome (SIDS) while under the care of marginal parents who functioned intellectually at a twelve-year-old level.

Austen, the infant's case manager, had come by his anxiety naturally. Months before the baby's birth, Austen had warned his supervisor about their challenges and questioned their capacity to parent, but in the past year the state's Child Protective Services mandated that families stay together, even when positive outcomes appeared questionable.

Austen's concerns fell on deaf ears. In this particular case, the psychologist who provided a comprehensive assessment and recommendations conveyed that these parents had a decent shot at keeping their baby. To that end, wraparound services such as in-home counseling and visiting health care had been initiated. The services were meant to guide and monitor families. Austen continued to identify child and family need, creating a comprehensive treatment plan to ensure child safety.

But in spite of the well-intentioned plan, Austen's two-month-old client had died. Did he believe it was the fault of the parents? Not necessarily. But he knew that infants were more vulnerable to SIDS if they were males, laid on their stomachs, and inhaled secondhand smoke. Austen had been apprehensive about little Troy's well-being because he knew Troy's parents chain-smoked and were unreliable when it came to consistently laying their baby on his back.

Austen's short-tempered supervisor was acutely aware of the political fallout that could occur as a result of an infant death, and from past experience Austen knew he was more likely to protect his own career by laying blame on Austen. When he entered his boss's office, Austen was bombarded with questions and asked why he hadn't raised greater opposition earlier to the parents' suitability to take care of their infant. Austen attempted several times to answer his superior, but was interrupted and told that whatever he had done on behalf of the child hadn't been enough.

Sensing his employee's vulnerability, his boss finished his remarks by icily stating, "You're probably not cut out for this work, my friend." Stung and humiliated, Austen barely remembers exiting. Thinking Austen weak and insecure, his boss had taken liberty with him.

The case manager wondered where things had gone so wrong. He was well aware that his state's Child Protective Services had shifted its focus several times over the years. Child-safety policies changed when state officials mandated one or the other of two opposite policies.

The first policy emphasized keeping children safe by removing them from their birth families and placing them in out-of-home care. The second policy centered on keeping children in their homes and embedding wraparound services. As political parties rotated power at the top of the state government food chain, a newly appointed child welfare secretary would predictably decide that the previous child welfare system, under his or her predecessor, was flawed. In addition, Austen also knew that money also drove political motives and dictated policy.

For over ten years Austen had been a dedicated worker. Then, a larger organization absorbed his agency into its own system of care. The new organization's business and social welfare practices had a negative impact on his morale. The larger system doubled Austen's paper work, and introduced an entirely new technical monitoring program. He discovered that, due to the corporate structure of the organization, policies were reviewed by layers of managers before final decisions were made about minor issues.

As a result of these changes, many of his coworkers jumped ship, but Austen felt loyal to clients, and even to his former agency. He had been lauded for his work in the past, and remained hopeful that he would be considered an asset by his new supervisor. He soon discovered his boss was hard-driving and ambitious, a man who had spent only two years in the field before he began his upward administrative climb.

Austen knew he had done his job but was extremely sad about the baby's death, mourning alongside the young parents. On the day of the funeral, he came back to his office and bumped into his boss, who neglected to acknowledge his presence or offer condolences. Austen felt invisible and defeated. The following day he submitted his resignation.

Bullies in the Workplace

Workplace bullying has always existed and, if considered at all, is largely viewed as a fact of life, part of getting the job done, and often a rite of workplace passage for new hires. Growing human enlightenment, workers' unions, and worker rights laws, have uncovered it to be an authentic problem; and yet it is still to be legislated within the United States.

Definitions of workplace bullying and the variation of it referred to as "mobbing" vary slightly. Workplace bullying is a verbal and behavioral, rather than a physical, form of violence against another worker. There is no single universal definition for workplace bullying, but in general, it refers to repeated use of aggressive or unreasonable behavior, which can include verbal attacks, threatening gestures, psychological behaviors, and abusive attitudes against coworkers. It is abuse that takes on overt or subtle forms.

Other sources define workplace bullying as a pattern of psychological and relational abuse over time, intended to degrade, humiliate, and isolate the bully's victim. Both types create serious damage, not only to the target, but to overall worker productivity at a huge cost to the workforce and employers.

Bullying may be affected by individual factors and/or corporate structure, with embedded practices and cultures. The Workplace Bullying Institute (WBI), an employee-advocacy group, states that nearly 50 percent of the U.S. workforce is either a victim of or a witness to bullying on the job. WBI's definition of workplace bullying is "repeated malicious mistreatment, verbal abuse, or conduct that is threatening, humiliating, or intimidating, or that interferes with work" (Workplace Bullying Institute, 2011). Bullying on the job is not the same as childhood bullying, but psychological and relational intimidation and threats are characteristics that they share. Examples include:

1. Verbal threats;

2. Offensive conduct, either verbal or nonverbal; threatening; humiliating; or intimidating; and

3. Sabotage or work interference that prevents work from getting done.

Mobbing vs. Bullying

Mobbing is similar to workplace bullying, in that it is an attempt to force someone out of the workplace through unmerited accusations, humiliation, general harassment, emotional abuse, and even terror. However, mobbing is broadened as "ganging up" by the leader or leaders, supervisors, coworkers, and/or subordinates who systemically collude to behave in "mob-like behavior" (Davenport, Distler Schwartz, & Pursell Elliott, 2005). While workplace bullying can result from a one-on-one exchange, mobbing generally includes two or more individuals.

Workplace bullying and mobbing are characterized by detrimental outcomes as a result of physical and/or psychological behavior on the part of the bully toward the target. Fallout from bullying ranges from the emotional toll of experiencing an uncomfortable and awkward work environment, to a target's inability to work again as a result of work trauma. The greatest tragedy occurs when someone commits suicide as a result of his or her experience with bullying/mobbing (Namie & Namie, 2009).

Common Misperceptions

The social service workplace has struggled with the concept of workplace bullying because, for all intent and purposes, it continues to hang on to antiquated precepts from the Old English Poor Laws, established five hundred years ago.

For example, the field still holds onto the Old English Poor Laws tenet regarding blame. Its premise states, "Change is inevitable in helping the poor, because efforts will soon be the subject of reform and criticized as insufficient." In other words, "we'll never get it right."

Consequently, misplaced blame weaves its way throughout social services. It's not a leap to assume that targets are often blamed when something goes wrong, and perceived to be weak individuals.

"Workplace Bullying or Mobbing Targets (Victims) Are Weak Individuals"

Workplace targets are often misperceived as being weak individuals, who need to grow thicker skins. Arguments lie in the assumption that the workplace is an inherently tough environment, especially in social services. To address the complex issues of the social service workplace, one must simply plow through challenges from clients, regulations, budgets, and contract managers, not to mention legislators. Within many social service organizations, bullying is accepted, and viewed as an okay way to blow off steam on the job. Individuals that hold to this belief assume that bullying is a subjective experience.

Are targets of bullying weak individuals, as some claim? Not according to a Workplace Bullying Institute and Zogby International Polling Survey (2007) that questioned over 7,700 adult Americans. According to the study, targets are more likely to endure stress in silence: 38 percent made an informal internal complaint, 15 percent filed a formal internal complaint, 4 percent filed a formal EEO complaint, 3 percent filed a lawsuit, but 40 percent suffered in silence.

The study also revealed that 73 percent of targets suffer for more than six months, 44 percent endure for more than one year, while 12 percent of the targets left their jobs.

"Workplace Bullies Are Not Dangerous"

Another common misperception is that workplace bullies are simply obnoxious people, but not really dangerous. There is, however, a difference between being an irritating coworker and a workplace bully. Bullies do real harm. Current initiatives to enact workplace anti-bullying state legislation submit that legal action against workplace bullying could occur if an employee's health is impaired or compromised when victimized on the job by a bully.

One way to distinguish between an irritating coworker and a bully might be the target needing to be prescribed medication to control elevated blood pressure or diabetes and/or modulate depression. At the far end of the spectrum, some individuals retire early owing to the risk of exacerbating their chronic conditions such as depression, heart disease, and diabetes, while others file for disability as a result of newly diagnosed health problems brought on by stress.

"Traditional Human Resource Training for On-the-Job Harassment Is Sufficient to Prevent Workplace Bullying"

One could argue that on-the-job ethics, cultural sensitivity, and conflict-resolution training provides workers with adequate tools to protect themselves from workplace bullying. But these workplace topics are taught to clarify behavior that does not violate existing state and federal discrimination laws that cost employers millions of dollars in lawsuits and settlement claims. Workplace bullying is not illegal, and the appropriate training will probably not occur until there are applicable state laws.

Unless bullying (harassment) is occurring on the basis of the target's gender, religion, national origin, or some other status protected under discrimination laws, employees have no legal course of action. The Civil Rights Act and other laws are not necessarily a panacea, but, to some extent, they have drawn a line and placed a spotlight on unacceptable behavior within the workplace.

In addition, ethics training is not necessarily guided by laws and doesn't sufficiently address the problem. Ethics is derived from both the Greek word *ethos*, which means character, and the Latin word *mores*, meaning customs. Ethics defines what is good for both society and individuals. Ethical standards are created to help professionals identify ethical issues in practice and provide guidelines in order to determine what is acceptable, or unacceptable, ethical behavior (Reamer, 1998). While the origins of law are often based on ethical principles, law does not prohibit all unethical behaviors. So while workplace bullying is unethical, it is still legal.

In addition, attorneys for employers may claim that the tort of "intentional infliction of emotional distress" (IIED) covers workplace bullying. However, it is almost impossible to prove under our current case law. It takes an enormous amount of evidence to prove that a defendant's conduct was so extreme and outrageous as to affect the health of a coworker.

"Workplace Bullying Consists of Manageable Conflicts Occurring Between Equals"

Workplace bullying has often been misperceived as two people with equal power engaged in an interoffice conflict that is easily negotiated through mediation. Bullying results in no visible cuts or bruises on the victim, but it is still psychological violence, instigated by one "side" against the target (victim), who is not in a position to respond with equal force. While power differentiation often equates to supervisor-supervisee scenarios, it can also occur with two people in parallel positions. For example:

Jennifer Wasn't Truly Jason's Equal, in Spite of Their Parallel Positions

Jennifer went to work in the human resources department of an elder-care organization. Initially, she and her coworker Jason got along, and she even related to him as a friend as well as a colleague.

Jason's first job out of college was at their agency, and as years passed, he worked hard to make himself indispensable to the organization. Unfortunately, Jason's training and current position did not preclude him from marginalizing people out of the workplace when they became professional threats. He carefully guarded his position where other talented people shared his work space. In addition, he was making more money than he had ever dreamed, and was worried that others would discover how much he was actually earning with bonuses.

Jennifer was talented and soon promoted to a parallel job within the department. Threatened by his perceived rival, Jason began to undermine her work by casually mentioning to their supervisor that Jennifer was "emotionally fragile." Jason demonstrated other mean-spirited behaviors in large meetings, which included rolling his eyes and giggling when her name was mentioned. He also spread erroneous rumors alluding to her being somewhat "slow" to grasp the work.

Eventually Jennifer caught wind of these rumors. Unaccustomed to submarine attacks from coworkers, she spent some time trying to wrap her head around Jason's behavior. At first she thought she'd misinterpreted coworker reports about his conduct, and asked him to help her out by clarifying her source's disclosures. In response to her query he became visibly upset and walked away without responding. Her additional attempts at communicating with Jason did not curb his behavior either. Jennifer began keeping a journal when she was blindsided by his actions, and requested through e-mail to meet with him to communicate her concerns and resolve the issue; still, no response.

When all else failed, she took her concerns to their boss who, over the months, had been given misinformation about her as well. As the vice president of human resources, he was at a loss as to how to categorize her comments, and pushed Jennifer in the wrong direction by telling her that there was nothing he could do about the situation. It was "Jason's word against hers," he stated.

Jennifer felt that she was caught between a rock and a hard place. A longtime employee, Jason was trusted by senior management. She feared that if she were to confront him again, he would file a harassment complaint.

Colleagues who initially disclosed Jason's behavior were unwilling to advocate for her because they reported to Jason, who already had management's ear. She knew managers were reluctant to risk losing someone who worked over sixty hours a week. She was also aware that Jason was desperate to keep his position and salary intact. Jennifer remained quiet, stayed to herself, and slowly lost her confidence.

As time passed, she was given fewer assignments and a smaller office in an isolated part of the building. As her work and morale declined, she also worried about losing her job. Her concerns were reflected in a newly diagnosed ulcer. When a new position at the organization became available she applied but was passed over. The job was given to a new worker with years less experience and knowledge. She translated the action as management's cue for her to leave.

Hindsight

Jennifer's bully had targeted her because he perceived her to be a threat. He used his power differential to make her look bad. Her boss failed to deal with the problem because he feared that if Jason left his job they would need to replace him with two people. Jennifer reflects on her experience and states, "I don't know if I will ever get over what happened to me. I have moved on but would love to see a few folks receive their due."

"Targets Create Their Own Problems"

Let's get this straight: Targets are not responsible for their mistreatment by bullies. Like its cousin, domestic violence, workplace bullying is now entering a new awareness cycle. Lack of money along with child care and job barriers weren't considered valid reasons why victims stayed with their abusive partners, and the same logic pertains to targets of bullying.

In the old days (meaning the last century), victims were often told by police officers and social workers that they were responsible and should simply leave their abusers. Much like domestic violence, abuse at work has inherited the same bias. An outdated perception still persists that workplace targets cause their abuse, and if bothered on the job should seek employment elsewhere. Workplace bullying is abuse, and should never be excused.

For instance, a supervisor goes on a rampage and verbally assaults his staff. His employees are taken by surprise, and everyone remains silent because they know he could turn on one of them. The next day, the boss apologizes. Newer workers accept his apology and trust he's sincere. At that moment, the abuser probably is sincere. Yet, veteran staff know an apology never ends his behavior. They wonder when his next explosion will occur, and at what cost to their morale and mental and physical health.

Similar to domestic violence victims, targets at work have family responsibilities and other challenges preventing them from leaving. And, after suffering years of abuse, they may have developed an erroneous belief that they are somehow flawed employees, as well.

Another analogy (that compares workplace bullying to domestic violence), includes the example of a program director who works diligently to write a grant proposal that is eventually awarded to his organization. The grant brings in millions of dollars, yet the boss doesn't recognize the director's contribution. The director continues to scramble to get his supervisor's attention, but it never happens.

In an effort to "do better" the employee continues to bring additional innovations to the organization, and continues to receive little recognition or appreciation from senior managers. Desperate for approval, our employee finally confronts his boss by questioning this lack of support. Instead of offering an apology, his superior responds by saying that if it hadn't been for the organization, the director would never have had an opportunity to "make a difference." No apology. All said and done, the director feels invisible and undervalued, much like a domestic violence victim who has worked like a dog to gain her partner's approval.

Workplace Bullying Laws

Workplace bullying, within the United States, does not fall under current workplace violence protections, although, technically, it is a form of violence. It is a form of nonphysical, psychological violence. Violence policies and laws focus on the acts and threats of physical violence, such as striking (battery) or threatening someone, to cause fear of being physically hurt (assaulted).

One exception is the inclusion of verbal abuse in violence policies. In only 20 percent of cases do antidiscrimination laws actually apply to workplace bullying. In order to claim sexual harassment, racial discrimination, or hostile work environment, the recipient of the mistreatment must be a member of a protected status group. This would not include a white female who is targeted by another white female.

Yet, there has been success. In 2008, the Indiana Supreme Court upheld a $325,000 verdict against a cardiovascular surgeon when a medical technician accused the surgeon of charging at him with clenched fists, screaming and swearing. The formal legal claims were "intentional infliction of emotional distress and assault," and the plaintiff argued it as a bullying case and had an expert on workplace bullying testify at the trial.

Again, at the time of this writing, there is no U.S. law against workplace bullying, and there is no plan to create a federal law to address workplace bullying. The United States is the last country among industrialized Western democracies to hold out. No state has enacted an anti-bullying law either. Although bills have been introduced by various states, laws passed by both houses in state legislatures and signed into law by the governor have not been enacted. Authors and psychologists Namie and Namie (2011) have spent years working to bring about workplace bullying awareness and have advocated for a Healthy Workplace Bill (HWB).

In addition, U.S. workers' rights advocates have been campaigning for years to get states to enact laws against workplace bullying. Those who oppose a workplace bullying law argue that should such a state law be passed, courts would be flooded with frivolous law suits. Yet, proposed bills in their definitions have required evidence of serious health harm or a pattern of negative employment decisions against a targeted individual. It would be difficult to defend bullies when their actions have caused cardiovascular disease or stress-related health complications in employees (The Healthy Workplace Campaign, 2010).

Other Countries and Workplace Bullying

The Swedish medical scientist Heinz Leymann in the latter part of the twentieth century founded the first international bullying movement, when he established a government-sponsored clinic to diagnose and treat workers suffering from what he called "psychological terrorization." Leymann labeled workplace bullying "mobbing," calling it a prolonged attack by a group of workers on a single colleague.

His work in the 1990s connected extremely hostile conditions in the workplace to post-traumatic stress disorder (PTSD). Because of his advocacy work, Sweden enacted the world's first national workplace safety and health ordinance (the Ordinance Concerning Victimization at Work), which identified and addressed bullying. It went into effect in 1994.

Worldwide Agreement

While their definitions are still not formalized, there is worldwide agreement that bullying and mobbing are repeated, uninvited covert or overt acts against another that lead to psychological and physical personal injury. The issue of workplace bullying and mobbing is recognized in Europe with Sweden, Norway, Finland, and Germany having enacted occupational safety laws that legally address this behavior. In addition, hotlines providing support for the problem have been established in the United Kingdom, Germany, Austria, and Switzerland (Davenport et al., 2005).

And, across the border, Canadian federal employees in 2008 became protected against bullying, under revised provisions of the national Occupational Health and Safety Regulations. The Canadian province of Quebec's Labour Standard went into effect in 2004 and outlawed psychological harassment at work. The provinces of Saskatchewan, Ontario, and Manitoba have also enacted health and safety regulation changes since, which address workplace bullying as a potential health hazard (Namie & Namie, 2011).

The Merry-Go-Round of Workplace Bullying and Social Services

The idea that bullies exist within the social services workplace may be difficult to wrap one's mind around. After all, looking after vulnerable people within our society is what makes us civilized. Rational thinkers could understandably assume that within the social services scope of helping others, people would be *more* compassionate and concerned for subordinates and coworkers. Yet, as stated in the first chapter, the system that promotes protection of society's less empowered happens also to set the stage for a perfect storm that incubates bullying in the workplace. As a matter of fact, the social service arena was identified as one of the top three areas of employment where workplace bullying exists (Namie & Namie, 2011).

At first blush, one might assume that bullying at work pertains to for-profit private corporations, whereas the issue of bullying within social services applies only to perpetrators who directly abuse children, spouses, or the elderly. And while abuse continues among society's vulnerable citizens, the social welfare workforce is replete with its own bullies. Bullying occurs in social services organizations, in spite of clearly written mission statements and guiding ethical principles that are prominently displayed in lobbies and embedded within donor materials.

Many social services agencies have incorporated "perpetrator-victim-rescuer" cultures that feed dysfunction. Policy makers, administrators, supervisors, ancillary human advocacy agents, and frontline workers change positions on this merry-go-round as policies are written, budgets and services negotiated, work assigned and supervised, and outcome-data collected.

One example includes government funding systems that have historically controlled and paid for social services. In transitional political climates and tough economic times, drastic shifts occur that include rotating or cutting funding in human services. As a result, politicians pit different social service providers against one another by prioritizing one service over another. For example, in one state, government leaders have prioritized funding for child protection, favoring it over other services such as substance abuse, mental health, and juvenile justice. Their plan ultimately creates tension between these service providers.

On the surface, children are the "neediest" group of clients—until one considers that parents of these kids need substance abuse and mental health intervention in order to do their job as caregivers. In addition, juvenile justice systems suffer because many neglected and abused incarcerated youth grow into angry and antisocial adults who may end up neglecting or abusing their own children. In ten years, legislators may decide that substance abuse should be more heavily weighted; and so the merry-go-round of entitlement continues.

Here is what it can look like:

The Social Service Funding Merry-Go-Round

Persecutor—State Government that continues to cut programs without examining true need,

and

Rescuer—Social Services Organizations that assist persons in need,

and

Victims—Clients who no longer receive necessary mental health medication or intervention services, substance abuse support, or adequate help for youth

morph into . . .

Persecutors—Clients who grow up to become chronically mentally ill, substance dependent, and/or neglectful and abusive parents,

and

Rescuers—State Government investigators that build larger facilities to address citizen safety and client control,

and

Victims—Social Services Organizations flooded with client need and reduced budgets . . .

Diagram B

This diagram illustrates the circle or flow of dysfunction (social dynamic) that occurs to create workforce bullying. These roles can shift into a former victim morphing into a persecutor as a former persecutor now assumes the role of a rescuer, while a former rescuer transforms into a victim.

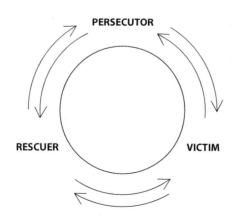

The Frontline Worker Merry-Go-Round

The frontline merry-go-round phenomenon happens when social workers strive to empower their clients. Sometimes their motives include unconscious impulses that relate to the word *rescue*. To complicate matters, clients being "saved" (also known as "victims") may believe themselves victimized by persecuting systems, such as housing authorities or law enforcement.

In time, clients may transform into persecutors when they push back against their well-intentioned helpers if they fail to meet client expectations. Formerly identified persecutors (the government, perhaps) now become client-perceived rescuers when they are mandated to step in to investigate the client's complaint. Former helper/rescuers now perceive themselves to be victims.

The Trickle-Down Effect

Bullying has also contributed to "dumbing down" social services. For example, laws and policies set by legislators and government agencies at the top dictate the majority of social service policies, budgets, and outcome measures. Policies change with new elections and leadership transitions. Lawmakers, who are, in general, not terribly interested in social welfare issues, leave social service administrators to struggle with bending to their hot-and-cold political agendas in state capitals.

Over time, these ever-transitioning government leaders can affect the quality of statewide program service delivery. Their shifting political agendas often put a halt to sound evidence-based programs, as when evidence-based care is trumped by non-evidence-based methodologies promoted by leaders who may owe people favors.

The Technology Connection

In the past thirty years, I've led social service–related trainings throughout the United States and other countries. Attendees represent a wide spectrum of professionals and paraprofessionals. And, over the years, I've become aware of a shifting workforce that has grown to pattern much of its behavior on the overall culture of technology.

Technology became a pivotal resource as accountability entered into the social welfare picture following, in some cases, years of fiduciary negligence. In certain instances, millions of dollars were thrown toward inefficient and disorganized social service organizations that lacked oversight or held administrators accountable. As a result, the pendulum swung the way of business models focused more on operations than evidence-based practice. And while new technology systems have added much to accountability and efficiency, they have also added to the cost of running social programs. (Information specialists working alongside social workers are now often earning larger salaries.)

The use of technology doesn't address relational gray areas that come with helping human beings. Further, the use of text messaging and e-mailing at work has cut back on face-to-face client interaction and created a new work culture filled with tech-savvy individuals who may have marginal skills when it comes to communication. Many workers who report on-the-job bullying mention receiving cryptic or mean-spirited directives online from their tech-savvy supervisors working only ten feet away.

While workplace culture has been created around technology, human relations communication has suffered. Many supervisors are no longer required to supervise in person. One worker, for instance, reported that her boss never leaves his office. Their communication is carried on through a "smart" phone that lacks a voice, eye contact, and body language. This woman's boss is socially backward but valued by his superiors for his technical skills. And no, he isn't the head of information technology. Sadly, his lack of knowledge and experience in working with children and families goes unrecognized by his superiors because he's in charge of program innovations.

While technology has gone a long way to improve data collection in social services, it has also contributed to the tension between organizational mission, supervision practices, and worker satisfaction. Managers have shifted more toward keeping their eyes on the ball through technology, in order to accommodate contract requirements and address mandated outcome measures tied to funding. Consequently, senior managers within social service organizations may have no background or training in the work provided by their agency. They are paid solely to focus on business operations, and simply don't have knowledge about delivering quality services. As a result, they may rely on assistants, who present their own recommendations with great conviction and charisma but lack the necessary education or experience to back them up.

A growing number of managers are business people, not trained in social services work, and clients have paid a price because shifting administrative practices have placed less emphasis on embedding evidence-based practices into their systems of care.

What Does This All Mean for Workplace Bullying?

Even as the social service work culture has changed, one fact remains the same: people want to be told, in person, that they are valued for their work contributions. The introduction of technology into social services leaves gaps in communication, and employees are left to guess, or assume, they're doing okay on the job. And, where there are interpersonal communication gaps at work, bullying grows, because bully behavior also engages in secrecy, innuendo, and rumor.

And, just as technology has had an impact on social service professionals, it has also reflected a change in social service leadership. Individuals who were once valued for their approaches to responsible social welfare practice have shifted and taken a back seat to administrators and supervisors now driven by data collection. The skills once valued in senior managers are no longer valued, when compared with current social services business practice.

Consequently, present-day administrators are more often valued for their political savvy and technical knowledge rather than client focus and consistency that support long-term evidence-based care for persons in need. Staying the course, and respectfully managing a workforce whose primary mission is to help others, indicates strong leadership.

Strong leadership is needed to address the workplace bullying problem. Without enlightened leadership, bullying in social services will occur. And it does.

Neighbors Living Worlds Apart
Bullies and Targets—Bullies

Bully's motto: "Let's get them before they get us."

Bully—"A person who hurts, frightens, or tyrannizes over those who are smaller or weaker."

Power—"The ability to control others, sway or influence."

Authority—"The power or right to give commands, enforce obedience, take action, or make final decisions." (*Webster's New World College Dictionary*, 1999)

Bad Behavior + One Whistle-Blower = Workplace Bullying

Lt. Paula Coughlin never wanted to be famous. She just wanted to do her job. She was considering all of the above as she walked briskly down the hall to the office of the United States Secretary of Defense. Following her meeting with the Secretary, she was to be escorted to the White House to meet with the president. To this day, she remembers hearing the sound of her heels clicking against the cold polished floor of the Pentagon as she approached the Secretary's office; crisp, echoing steps. Arriving at her destination, the then-Secretary glared at Lt. Coughlin and stated that because of her, he had to accept the Secretary of the Navy's resignation. He could just have easily have said, "Thank you for what you've done for your country Lieutenant."

Let's start at the beginning . . .

In September of 1991, the 35th Annual Tailhook Symposium was held at the Hilton Hotel in Las Vegas, Nevada. Since their first get-together, in 1956, these symposiums had become increasingly rowdy, and the acts of indecency and molestation that resulted at this particular year's conference, followed by the official responses to the event, have become known as the Tailhook Incident.

The Tailhook Association is a private, nonprofit social/professional organiza-tion of naval aviators, contractors, and others involved in naval aviation. In the past, the U.S. Navy had consistently provided significant support and cooper-ation to the conference and to the Association. While concerns had been shared about attendee behavior by Navy and Association personnel, no actions had yet been taken to rein in their grossly inappropriate behaviors. According to the official inquiry into the events of Tailhook (February, 1993), from Thursday, September 5, 1991 through the early morning hours of Sun-day, September 8, 1991, at least ninety people were victims of some form of indecent assault. Of that number, eighty-three were women and seven were men. Their ages ranged from eighteen to forty-eight, and eight victims were assaulted more than once. One lone female, Lt. Paula Coughlin, emerged as this story's hero, but at great professional and personal cost.

Lt. Coughlin was a thirty-year-old Admiral's Aide and helicopter pilot when she entered the third-floor hallway of the Hilton Hotel that fateful weekend. Upon her entry, someone began to yell, "Admiral's Aide!"

It began. She was grabbed on the buttocks from behind and lifted off the ground. As she turned to confront the man, another man came from behind and grabbed her buttocks again. She was pushed into the crowd of men who collectively began pinching her body and pulling at her clothing. Her breasts were grabbed and someone else reached underneath her skirt to grab her panties. Paula states, "I felt as if the group were trying to rape me." As she saw one of the men in the group walk away, she reached out and tapped him on the hip, pleading with him to "just let me get in front of him." The man turned around to face her, raised his hands, and placed them on her breasts.

To say that Paula's assailants' actions were unbecoming to officers is an under-statement. Yet, mustering great courage, the lieutenant cracked the code on the power differential within the Navy when she filed an official complaint of assault within one month following the incident.

Secretary of the Navy H. Lawrence Garrett III, took the first official action. He directed the Navy to end all support for the Tailhook Association, which in 1991 included providing free office space and transporting Navy officers to the annual conference at an estimated cost of $400,000. One week later, the Chief of Naval Operations removed the commander of Patuxent River Naval Air Test Center for "his apparent failure to take timely and appropriate action" when his aide, Lt. Paula Coughlin, reported to him her abuse at Tailhook '91. She states,"I messed up his day when he learned about my assault and made it clear he didn't agree with 'what I did to all the senior staff.'"

But the full investigation promised by the Navy Secretary failed to materialize. And the first Tailhook Report in 1992 was found to be incomplete due to the fact that there had been a large-scale lack of cooperation on the part of the officers and their commanding officers. It was also discovered that the Naval Investigative Service (NIS) failed to include in its final report fifty-five pages of interviews, one of which placed Navy Secretary Garrett at the scene of many of the indecent assaults that occurred at the Symposium.

So where does Lt. Coughlin's workplace bullying and mobbing come into play, when sexual assault is obviously against the law?

As a result of her formal complaint, a negative whispering campaign had started against the young lieutenant. In addition, her mounting frustration over the Navy's lack of action almost one year following the incident compelled her to publicly identify herself in late June of 1992, and describe her attack in press interviews. In response to the articles and news stories about her, the White House requested and received Secretary Garrett's resignation. The Tailhook report summarized,"There was a serious breakdown in leadership at Tailhook '91. Leaders in naval aviation, ranging from the squadron commanders to flag officers, who tolerated a culture that engendered the misconduct, also share a portion of the blame" (February, 1991).

The Tailhook Legacy

What Does Tailhook Mean?

Tailhook refers to the hook located on the bottom of the aircraft that captures the cable on the flight deck in order to slow down the aircraft when it lands on an aircraft carrier. Individuals who have landed an aircraft or been onboard when an aircraft landing occurred become a member of the Tailhook Association. They are invited to attend an annual Navy Tailhook professional symposium. At the time of the Tailhook Incident in 1991, this annual symposium had morphed into a male bonding ritual that included heavy drinking, exploiting women, and otherwise engaging in indecent behaviors.

Bullies on Steroids

Lt. Coughlin had, in essence, called out the Good Old Boy military system and the guys didn't like it one bit. Remarks by fellow male officers such as "You f**d up the whole Navy" were common.

People who blow the whistle in the workplace easily become bullying targets. And while her case was in process, Paula continued to work as an aviator for four more years. During that period, she was treated with disdain and shunned by people she'd previously considered friends.

Whistle-blowers have been given a bad rap, mostly because they've stepped outside the conformity box, prompted by their conscience and their desire to right a wrong. But it is more often the whistle-blowers than the wrongdoers who are isolated and punished by supervisors and coworkers. "There were very few days I didn't cry on my way to and on my way home from work," Paula remarks. At one point she was able to move closer to her family, where she received loving support, particularly from her boyfriend, who would become her husband. He checked newspapers daily before he gave Paula the go-ahead to read them, fearing one more derogatory editorial or letter to the editor about her.

Over time, the stress Paula experienced began to compromise her health, and she acquired sinus infections, gained and lost weight, and drank more wine than she should have. When she did receive counseling, she spent time in sessions feeling validated and flagging military system discrepancies that centered on her rights. Yet, she was not comforted by the fact that, because she was in the military, all her medical records were military property and HIPAA confidentiality rules did not apply.

Her copilots continued to ascribe to what is called "professionalism in the cockpit," but once away from the aircraft, became part of the mobbing culture. Eventually Paula acquired an ulcer and her mental well-being suffered. She was prescribed Zoloft and grounded from flying. At a particularly low point she considered taking her life because "it seemed like the best solution for everyone."

As her case began to sort itself out, Paula knew she needed to leave the military. She had hoped to make it a career but, after ten years, she'd had enough. Eventually, she won her sexual assault case against the Las Vegas Hilton, where the incident took place.

Now, after two decades, with biographies written and a TV movie titled *She Stood Alone* based on her experience, Paula reflects, "My children still don't know the impact my experience had on me, and I'm living a completely different life. But there are so many things service organizations can do to prevent something like this from happening. We're wasting talent, time, and energy when someone harms someone else."

Some retired and current military persons contend that Lt. Coughlin knew what she was doing when she walked down that hallway in 1991. They are careful to say that while her assailants had no right to molest her, she knew what she was getting herself into. Their assertions are based on flawed thinking, because they are based on ignorance. And ignorance always reveals itself. For example, these are the same judgments made when civil rights workers sat at all-white lunch counters, or when Gandhi demonstrated peacefully against British colonial rule. There are few people willing to take a bullet standing up to injustice. Former Lt. Paula Coughlin is a hero to all military persons.

One might also ask how social services and Paula's military background relate to each other. Sexual assault is a social welfare concern and is normally addressed by social services organizations. It could be said that the United States Armed Forces is the largest social services system in the world, because it serves to protect its citizens. This does not preclude protection for those harmed from within their own organization. The military must protect all U.S. citizens from inside, as well as outside, its borders (Paula Coughlin, personal communication, May 20, 2011).

Social Service Workplace Bullies

Defined in Chapter 2, bullying occurs where there is an imbalance in real or perceived power between the bully and the target. For example, in the case of Tailhook, Lt. Coughlin was well beneath the power equivalent of her admiral. And in her case, he chose to use his power to stonewall the investigation. Lt. Coughlin followed proper procedures, but those with more power took advantage of their status until the truth came publicly to light.

Bullying could also be defined as "actualized arrogance" that affirms the power needs of the abuser, and takes advantage of the vulnerability of the victim, particularly when there is a lack of support that leaves the target feeling isolated and exposed, often with lasting consequences that include damaged self-esteem. Again,

Lt. Coughlin's bullies were demonstrating marked arrogance in their attitudes and behaviors toward her.

Bullies feel contempt for their targets, often considering them to be worthless, inferior, or undeserving of respect. Signs of contempt for another range from disregard to scorn or hate. Bullies exclude, isolate, segregate, or bar targets from participating fully in the workplace. The victims, whether male or female, were held in contempt by their aggressors at the '91 Symposium.

Bullies often feel entitled because of their power positions and organizational relationships with people in power. They view themselves privileged to control, dominate, and subjugate others. And, depending on their worldview, normally incubated in childhood, they have acquired intolerance for persons and situations that do not share their particular beliefs. They may even have a completely different perspective about their professional mission versus that of their organization. Consequently, targets who do not subscribe to their way of thinking are not worthy of their respect.

Bullies have:

- The power to exclude the target victim who is viewed as unworthy,

- The feeling of entitlement and privilege to control and dominate another person, and

- Intolerance for differences (in other words, "difference" means inferior and not worthy of respect)

Given certain circumstances, anyone can morph into a bully. But some people are more predisposed to it than others. Aggression is a basic biological state in humans, and certain factors can increase levels of aggression beyond acceptable norms. High levels of testosterone in men, for example, can encourage aggressive behavior that inflicts harm and leads to antisocial behaviors. Higher levels of testosterone have been found even in preschool bullies (Beane, 2008). In addition, as biological creatures, when humans perceive threat, their arousal systems go into action and prepare them to defend themselves through aggression, withdrawal, submission, or freezing behaviors.

When bullies are threatened, their arousal response normally operates at the aggressive or withdrawal level. Threats aren't perceived as physical by adult bullies. Much of their perception depends on how transference, a psychological process that triggers an unconscious response when prompted by sensory stimulation, takes them "down memory lane."

Transference prompts an unconscious reaction to someone because of what a person (in this case, the bully) needs to see in order to feel less threat, fear, and insecurity. Bullies project characteristics onto another person, even when they know very little about their target. For example, in Chapter 2, Austen became his boss's "fall guy" because Austen's calm demeanor was perceived as weakness by his supervisor, who then felt free to be intimidating and verbally abusive. Austen may as well have worn an "invisibility cloak."

Transference is psychological projection usually caused by unmet emotional needs, neglect, seductions, and other abuses that occurred in earlier life. Transference causes bullies to misread someone, and then react negatively. The perpetrator-victim-rescuer merry-go-round, described in Chapter 2, can exacerbate existing workplace bullying cultures when leadership and supervision patterns get played out repeatedly by unaware participants (bullies in this case) who project their prior experiences onto coworkers.

"Projection" is projecting one's own feelings, emotions, and/or motivations onto another without recognizing that one's projections are truly about one's self. For example, in social services, a bully supervisor transfers memories of his father's alcoholism to his job, when he verbally "puts down" subordinates who sympathize with the disease of addiction, calling them "bleeding hearts."

In other cases of projection, female coworkers participate in mobbing a new, attractive female coworker because she reminds them of their high school experiences with popular girls. They project their high school rejection onto their target even though they know nothing about her (Conner, 2007). The end result is psychological alienation at work.

When bullying goes unidentified, and occurs repeatedly in social services organizations, chances are leadership has also morphed into one large organism where management shares the same worldview, and very often childhood problems. One reported COO and CEO both had alcoholic fathers and strong, tough-minded resilient mothers. The two bonded over their early life experiences, and grew up perceiving that women were unacceptable leaders if they appeared emotional or less aggressive. These guys confused quiet strength with blatant weakness. As a result, they hired female senior managers just like their moms. Their management styles and personalities were fused. In this particular organization, the softer spoken qualified female applicants were passed over because they were perceived as weak.

Real or perceived threats cause stress, prompting heightened arousal within human beings. Heightened arousal can trigger survival reactions. As we know, stress can be positive or not; depending on how it compels us toward, or away from, something. When bullies perceive someone as a threat, their arousal systems go into gear and their survival reactions are either to become aggressive or to avoid the person altogether, and they may use underhanded methods to target their victims.

In addition, social services administrators and supervisors normally dictate the manner in which conflicts are resolved in the workplace. For example, administrator bullies who deal with their stress by becoming aggressive will, consciously or unconsciously, give permission to their management team to behave in the same manner. This approach is more transparent and pretty blatant.

On the other hand, administrator bullies who use avoidance as a way to deal with stress will role-model resolving conflict behind closed doors. This can be a very dysfunctional way to run an organization. It more or less leaves people in the dark, wondering when the next shoe will drop. Issues get resolved in a closed parallel universe where gossip, innuendo, and marginal ethics are played out. This is how dysfunctional social structures are created.

Are Bullies Deeply Disturbed Human Beings?

Do bully actions reflect severe personality disorders? While their targets would want to claim them as megalomaniac psychopaths, the overwhelming majority of bullies are not. And, unless they blatantly break the law or otherwise commit gross unethical acts, bullies do not have antisocial personalities either. Only a small percentage of workplace bullies could be diagnosed with antisocial personality disorder (Namie & Namie, 2011).

However, narcissistic individuals are more likely to be bullies. Someone with a narcissistic personality exhibits a pattern of grandiosity, need for admiration, and, most importantly, lack of empathy (American Psychiatric Association, 1994).

Narcissists truly believe themselves to be more special than the rest of the population and have acquired an inflated sense of self-importance. And they generally bond with one another. In other words, people who form a mobbing consortium are more likely to receive comfort by admiring each other; one could even say their own reflections. They may agree they're especially smart, witty, talented, and correct in their shared worldviews.

With regard to work, narcissists tend to believe they are the only ones who can run their organizations, understand clients, pull together budgets, and be seen as visionaries. No one reports his or her own accomplishments as persuasively as a narcissist.

Narcissists, in general, don't like to "hang out" with "regular folks" unless the focus is on them. They totally buy into their own projections and perceptions. Their thinking may settle on any of the following proposed thoughts and beliefs about their targets:

"You're not assertive enough" (translation: "You're weak")

"You're not as smart as me" (translation: "I'm the smartest")

"You haven't worked here long enough" (translation: "I've got more power")

"You couldn't do my job" (translation: "Don't even try")

"You're not part of our team" (translation: "You can't be in my club")

"You're too much of a <u>fill in the blank</u>" (translation: "You're weak")

"You haven't paid your dues, so you're not entitled" (translation: "I'm entitled")

"You're more of an independent contributor to the organization" (translation: "I'm the visionary")

"You're too weak" (translation: "You're not assertive enough, but I don't really want you to be")

"I make more money" (translation: "I have higher status")

"You're not socially on par with me" (translation: "We are not equals")

"You're too young, or too old" (translation: "We are not equals")

"You're not as attractive, or as physically fit as me" (translation: "We are not equals")

Often, Machiavellian (characterized by craftiness and deceit, and based on the book *The Prince* by the fifteenth-century Florentine statesman and writer Niccolò Machiavelli) in their behaviors, narcissistic bullies will usually spend time with supervisees for their own gain. Narcissists can be very aggressive, and are not above exploiting others; and in social welfare, use the excuse that it's better for the overall good of the organization.

According to authors Namie and Namie, bullies have excellent political skills. They "deserve to have others beneath them play a role in their grand design" (Namie & Namie, 2011). Unfortunately, these workplace bullies do not care if they psychologically crush their targets, because they have a strong propensity for rationalizing what they do.

Myths about Bullies

1. Bullies are loners—Nope. Most bullies are not socially isolated. They normally have at least a small group of friends who support and/or encourage them. Many have strong family ties and are active in their communities.

2. Bullies have low self-esteem—Not necessarily. While they may have unresolved childhood psychological wounds, narcissists believe themselves somewhat superior to those of us living on the ground floor (U.S. Department of Health and Human Services, 2010).

Who Does the Bullying and Who Gets Bullied?

It's no surprise that many bullies are people working in upper levels within vertically structured organizations. Executives have the title, power, and authority to start the ball rolling downhill.

Interestingly, the Workplace Bullying Institute and Zogby International Polling Survey (2007) found that half of the bullying occurs in front of witnesses. Male bullies (57.8%) prefer public bullying more than female bullies (48.6%), while females preferred abusing behind closed doors (47.2% vs. 38.3%). Sixty percent of bullies are men, and the majority of targets are women (57%). In 71 percent of reported cases, women target women, two and a half times more than men; but men target both genders, with a slight preference for males.

While managers and supervisors are more likely to bully, they are not immune from being targets themselves. New management or executives can be targeted when they enter a new work environment having been hired to change the culture in some way. Old-timers are often very skilled at making life miserable for the new guys. It's been known to happen that directors have been forced out within a short period of time because people resisting change knew how to get "bigger fish" to listen, simply owing to long-standing relationships. Often, the mere presence of someone unknown is threat enough to formulate exaggerated and uninformed complaints about a new employee. In addition, county official or other governing councils in community-run social services organizations often think they can do the job as well as the new leader or expert they've just hired. But when these folks (big fish) are contacted by the veteran employees, they may very likely change their minds and stand with their longtime community buddies. Again, existing dysfunctional social structures play a huge role in fueling the merry-go-round.

Why Do Bullies Target Others?

Many workplace bully experts would approach this question by simply answering, "Because they can, period, end of sentence." However, bullying in the helping arena has many layers; after all, the people there who bully were usually drawn to the profession because they wanted to help society's most vulnerable people. In general, they have a desire to make a difference. Much of the time, though, their decision to enter the helping profession had even more to do with an unconscious need to resolve personal childhood issues. Consequently, bullies in the social services workplace must step through and/or bypass personal awareness that would remind them why they became social welfare advocates in the first place. Their ability to overlook flaws within can be at a depth of 20,000 leagues. These folks very likely passed on self-awareness training that may have prompted them to examine their own intentions and behaviors. And, in fact, many social service bullies view personal process work as pointless and a sign of weak character.

True, there are some "organic" bullies, folks who have stepped on, mistreated, and made fun of others since preschool. A bad temper is a characteristic of childhood bullies, and unless harnessed, child bullies can grow up to be impulsive and explosive adults as well. When bullying behaviors are practiced and reinforced over years, it is very difficult to change those behaviors. Chronically inclined toward bullying, they not only bully on the job, but in the outside world as well. They're rude to servers, disrespectful to their mail carriers, and mean-spirited with their spouses and parents.

Narcissistic bullies also perceive themselves to be experts about almost everything at work. It doesn't matter if they know nothing about technology or counseling practice; they still believe they're right. Not only do bullies in the social service workplace see themselves as human rights supporters, they disdain anyone who has a different opinion.

Conformity plays a large role in the current bullying culture. In other words, if someone is not capable or willing to adapt to the agency's view (meaning the controlling view) about what "helping" means in the workplace, then that someone can be perceived by a bully to be a threat. For this reason, many targets are people who happen to be more nonconforming types. Nonconformists are normally folks who ask why the emperor wears no clothes.

In a bullying culture, where the tyranny of one right way can prevail, nonconformists are often treated with suspicion, and perceived as threatening the stability of the environment. Their presence can be disruptive when there is workplace inertia. Many times nonconformists are allowed to continue in their jobs but not brought into the inner circle and treated as decision makers. And within vertically structured organizations, nonconformists may be viewed as risky characters because they generally follow a personal code of ethics, and could "go off the reservation" when marginal practices are enacted in the course of doing business.

As mentioned earlier in this book, there is often a fine line between Saturday night and Sunday morning as it pertains to the separation between victims, perpetrators, and rescuers in the social services world. The person victimized today may be the perpetrator tomorrow, depending on the communication route followed and transposed by those in charge. For example, a supervisor bully in social services may be called on the carpet by her boss because a politician has called the boss to say a client complaint has been made to his office about the supervisor. The boss could then begin to target the supervisor because he believes the supervisor has put him at risk for being unpopular with the politician.

Bullies normally love being in control and controlling other people. Their worldview can be narrowed down to one phrase: "The one on top wins." Bullies are often the "climbers" in the workplace, and are adept at playing politics.

One bullying trick is for the bully to allow a target to speak first, having already rehearsed his or her message before the conversation. Similar to a cat toying with a mouse, the bully will then pounce, delivering a devastating remark to a target.

There can be a degree of sadism in bullies, in that they often enjoy seeing their targets become uncomfortable during these conversations. It's empowering for them. Surprise is a common bullying tactic. A conversation with a target might go something like this:

Bully: "What did you think of how you handled talking with the school principal about our counseling program?"

Target: "Well, I think it went pretty well. I know I still need to work on getting them onboard, but it's coming along great."

Bully: "Interesting—I've decided to take over those meetings from now on. Thanks. I've got to get to my meeting now."

Always considering their next political move on the workplace "Game Boy," bullies are astute in sizing up their competition. "Let's figure this out together" is not in their vocabulary. It's more like "This is the way it's going to happen." Bullies will go above and beyond to assess where the power lies within the organization, and stay connected to that source through a lot of bootlicking. They will engage the boss to be their mentor, and viciously guard their power positions. Bullies are especially attentive to human resources staff, and consider them strong influencers at work. Owing to the need to control and gain power, potential bully leaders in social services are as cutthroat as any group on Wall Street. As a matter of fact, one social services administrator, a former corporate V.P., mentioned that she witnessed more respectful behavior and professionalism in the for-profit corporate world.

While competition is a driving force behind bullying behavior, being bested by another employee becomes a war of survival. This story provides an example.

The Bulldog Policies: Strategies of a Donut-Maker-Turned-Bully

This story could also be called "How to Powder Your Own Donuts." Here, a former target relates her story, in her own words:

"I have observed others bullied and have been bullied on the job. Prior to my knowledge and understanding of the characteristics of workplace bullying I was somewhat apprehensive to do anything working in the human resources department as a human resources director.

"The first time I recall witnessing workplace bullying was at an employment advertising company where the owner/president victimized, manipulated, and inflicted emotional distress on many of the employees. When I confronted the bully, his comment to me was to stay out of his business or leave. I left as soon as I could land another position. My instinct was to get out as soon as I could.

"As a victim, working for a nonprofit social services organization, I was bullied by my boss, the aforementioned donut maker, who was vice president of human resources. But her change from benign supervisor to bully was gradual. This meant that the behavior did not start out blatant and clear. It began slowly and increased over a period of time, becoming more and more prevalent and routine. By the end of my employment, my boss went to every extreme to encourage my resignation. As long as she had a need of my talents and skills, she used and abused them. Once she no longer had the need, she went through every effort to discard me. I eventually left, but feeling terribly scarred for the following reasons.

"I first observed her treating coworkers the same. It was brutal. I chose to believe this could not happen to me until it did. For a period of time I was in denial. I felt my confidence in my abilities reduced. I am confident in my own skills and abilities, but this little person almost turned me into mush. I ended up fighting back in my own way. I started standing up for myself.

"I called her out on her actions. I identified work I developed after she had taken ownership. Instead of allowing her to steal my work and identify it as her own, I spoke up and would embarrass her by asking questions about the process that she would not know unless she developed it. This of course did not sit well with her, and I knew that it would be a matter of time before I would need to leave or she would find a way to remove me as she did others. There are many examples over my almost eight years of employment with this employer. This person is still employed there and as far as I know, still causing grief and distress to her victims" (personal communication, April 7, 2011).

The target in the above story had been an effective and loyal worker, developing and implementing many innovations. As she grew in recognition and skill, her bully became intimidated, and proceeded to downplay those accomplishments. By the end of her tenure, the target had been moved to a small office on the other side of the building, while her job tasks were reduced in scope and function.

Other Reasons People Bully

Money also drives bullies in social services. For example, social services adminis-trators routinely earn more than six figures a year with additional bonuses and benefits. In one organization, bully leaders and senior management were given a 20 percent pay raise after cutting staff and freezing raises for two years. Lower-level staff were finally given a 2 percent cost of living increase after months of assuming the workload left behind when their coworkers had been let go. This organization's board members had probably been given the message that the "bosses" had saved the organization from imminent financial ruin. Bullies survive at other people's expense.

Jealousy drives much bully behavior. Adult bullies are often motivated by besting anyone who threatens to "move or remove their cheese," and are easily threatened by competition or someone they perceive to have skills that might compete with what they have brought to the table. The target's story above is a great example. Other factors that drive on-the-job jealousy include comparing another's finances, luck, family life, and likeability with one's own circumstances.

Mentioned earlier in this chapter, fear drives many people to behave poorly. Whether they fear losing their job, power, or economic status, it underlines much of their bad behavior. Bullies in leadership (and climbing toward leadership) want to protect their self-image and restrict their contact with those they perceive as hav-ing the potential to make them look bad in the eyes of the powers that be, or who might threaten their status by appearing too "good."

Revenge can also urge on bullying and mobbing behavior. Here are some behavior examples:

- A subordinate inadvertently makes his boss look bad at a staff meeting; the boss then feels compelled to make life miserable for the unsuspecting target.

- A worker is given a promotion and begins to bully her former peers.

- In a meeting, Jerry asks a question that could paint the organization in a poor light, and his boss, without providing a reason, bars him from attending any more meetings.

- A childhood target, a bully makes up for her past misery by projecting her resentment onto employees who resemble her former bullies.

> **The Power of Tears**
>
> Female bullies can be very deceptive when they conjure up tears as a way to manipulate their supervisors and weep their way to power. In one instance, one woman routinely checked in with a powerful community figure and cried on his shoulder when she was called on the carpet for her unprofessional behavior. I watched this situation unfold in a county-run mental health program. The woman was one of the craziest mental health directors on earth, but she was crazy like a fox. It didn't hurt that she was powerfully attractive and men were drawn to her. Her sponsor was a very vulnerable, recently divorced community "mover and shaker," and obviously felt like a hero when he could intercede on her behalf. Sadly, she ruined many careers before her departure.

In addition, some individuals, not usually inclined toward bullying, become stressed at work and transform into bullies as a response to job tension. When things quiet down, and they've had a chance to gather their wits about them, they recognize the huge price they've paid in lost worker confidence and relationships.

Other bullies are just plain biased against certain cultures, personality types, genders, religions, and so on. They tend to overlook cultural diversity training at their social services organizations by hiring people like themselves. This practice further promotes workplace inertia.

Bullies emerge through social influences on the job as well. Like high school, the workplace can also be a hotbed for gossip, preferential friendships, and exclusion. Bullies desire to be in the popular crowd, viewing folks at the top as the popular ones. When someone is on the outs, such as a target, bullies will quickly jump on the bandwagon to make that person look even less attractive. Bullies are discriminating when it comes to favoring others. Bully favorites will be given glowing recommendations, sent notes of condolences, and otherwise included in after-hours socializing. Pity the many individuals that, by virtue of their humility, or lack of perceived status, get bullied and/or passed over as a work friend. Sadly, this practice also promotes psychological alienation on the part of the target.

> A true quote:"I don't just want to win. I want to crush them!"
>
> —Social services organization chief operating officer

The Methods of Their Madness—How Bullies Abuse

According to the WBI-Zogby survey (2007) the top-ten bullying tactics include:

1. Blaming a target for bully's errors—"Your job is to check my work!"

2. Unreasonable demands—"I don't care if you just received the grant request for proposal. You have a week to write the proposal so that I can have plenty of time to review it when I come back from vacation."

3. Criticism of ability—"You really don't have a knack for people-pleasing do you?"

4. Inconsistent Rule Compliance—"How do you know Annabelle was given the interview questions in advance?"

5. Threatening job loss—"Whenever we have to look at cutbacks your name goes up on the board."

6. Insults and put-downs—"Don't speak if you don't know what you're talking about."

7. Discounting and denying the target's accomplishments—"So what if you wrote the book, Forsythia is in operations and should chair that initiative."

8. Exclusion, or "icing" the target out—"We had a great time at the dinner party. We talked a lot about work. You weren't there were you?"

9. Yelling and screaming—"Just do what I say and I don't want to hear any more about it! What are you, stupid?"

and

10. Stealing credit—"I was able to increase our income last year by 20 percent because of our newly funded grant." (Which, by the way he didn't write.)

Other bully behaviors include:

> Engaging in obstructive behavior over time—"Do you mind if I sit in on the meeting with you, and listen to what you have to say? I'll probably add something as well."

> Gossiping or spreading rumors about the target—"Don't say anything, but she's not really going to be here much longer."

> Manipulation—"I was wondering if you could show me your notes on that operations plan for your innovation when we go to lunch tomorrow."

> Failing to communicate—"Oh, I'm sorry. I thought you were on vacation. I didn't think it mattered anyway."

> Other forms of intimidation—"If you leave, you can never come back to this organization."

> Intent to cause pain or personal distress—"Don't you understand? I don't care about your stupid project!"

In addition:

- 53 percent of surveyed individuals stated that they experienced verbal abuse, threats, humiliation, and intimidation.

- 45 percent of surveyed individuals stated they experienced interference with performance.

- 47 percent of surveyed individuals stated they experienced abuse of authority.

- 30 percent of surveyed individuals stated they experienced destruction of their relationships.

Cyber-Bullying at Work

Cyber-bullying is very subtle, and is associated with leaving someone out of the communication loop. "Didn't you get my e-mail? I sent it two weeks ago," is an excuse used by bullies. Or, "I didn't respond to your e-mail because I haven't had time. And, while we're on the subject, I think it rude of you to question me when you know I'm so busy." Any form of harassment online can be called on the carpet by human resources, so individuals who bully via the computer are more or less doing it by the process of elimination, to cut someone out of the communication.

Texting or e-mailing has been used to talk about coworkers behind their backs, and when used to communicate false information or otherwise sabotage another's work, it can be quite destructive to a target's career.

Bullies will also text one another during meetings, again leaving targets out of their world by bypassing communication. During one-on-one meetings, bullies will be disrespectful of their targets by continuing phone conversations or texting during a conversation. The intentions are to use technology as a wall between the bully and the target.

Reining in the Barbarians

Employers, in the ideal social services delivery world, should rein in bullies, but that doesn't happen when they intentionally or vicariously participate in the bullying by virtue of the organization's management structure, workplace inertia, or other existing policies.

For example, when John Bolton was nominated to be the ambassador to the United Nations, a former subordinate told the Senate that Bolton was a "serial abuser" and stated that he was a "kiss-up, kick-down sort of guy" (Cohen, 2010).

Is bullying evil? One would argue that willfully and with premeditation inflicting harm on a coworker without remorse at least verges on evil. To enjoy bullying is evil. But bullies don't see themselves as evil, because they rationalize their cause (whatever it is) as just.

Bullies would even probably agree that there is empathy erosion in today's overall society. And, they might even be appointed to serve on a special committee to examine the problem. Yet, when it comes down to their daily behavior and intentions, they don't have a leg to stand on. Bullying is evil. It is what it is.

The "Poster Gal" for Workplace Targets

My motto: "Me, myself, and why?"

This Is Where It Gets Personal

I've always believed that expecting the world to treat you fairly is like expecting a bull not to charge because you are a vegetarian. When I entered the social service field I was somewhat idealistic but never imagined myself the guardian of the human-transformation garden, and never expected it to be a bed of roses.

In this line of work there are bound to be a few bumps in the career road. It comes with the territory in any job, and especially when one works in social services. Human beings are tough, kind, unpredictable, brave, and not one, the same. So it goes without saying, that I've learned a lot over the years. Yet nothing prepared me for being targeted at work.

I share my story, with the hope that others, who may be questioning their own targeting experience, don't feel like they're going nuts, and perhaps learn from the erroneous assumptions I made about workplace bullying.

My Adventures in Oz

I started working as a social worker in Ohio more than three decades ago. The county social service was led by a dedicated man focused on helping children and families move past their problems. He knew all the employees personally, and had an open-door policy. And while he hadn't earned an MBA, he operated within budget and successfully tackled the operations side of the business. Budgets, in those days, included funding for training and professional development, prompting us to take advantage of workshops led by national social services innovators.

In addition, when issues between coworkers surfaced, our director was an impartial mediator. His respect for staff was appreciated, and it set the tone for how we comported ourselves at work. When external social services providers or clients raised concerns, he was present to resolve the problems, while making sure that none of his staff was harassed or bullied. We knew he had our backs.

My direct supervisor at this organization was well trained and professional, usually introducing her supervision sessions by saying something like, "My goal is for you to become better than me, at what we do." And while data gathering was addressed, face-to-face time with children and parents was stressed more. Regular case and peer supervision were built into the work schedule. We didn't carry laptop computers or cell phones while making home visits. We literally sat and talked with children and families without texting, telephoning, or otherwise disrupting our time together. Home visits lasted more than an hour, with the intention of monitoring child safety, but also of building relationships.

I've shared my earlier experience not to say that everything was perfect in "the good old days," but to highlight the fact that social service work environments have dramatically changed.

Fast forward to the twenty-first century . . .

Twenty-seven years later I work in another state at a large, nonprofit child-welfare agency, as the corporate director for their clinical initiatives. The organization is huge, with an annual budget of over 100 million dollars. It consists of service divisions spread across the state, and includes several executive directors, approximately a few thousand staff members, and a corporate administrative office, centrally located to include a corporate CEO, COO, CFO, vice presidents, and functional directors. This organization's management is vertically structured with an operations focus.

As I settled into this agency it slowly dawned on me that there were almost as many support personnel as frontline workers. Focus is on contract compliance with internal and external policies and procedures, which translates to a largely data-driven work culture. Clients still figure in the picture, but in my view, the focus of running the organization had become lopsided in the direction of operations. A balance between clinical and operational functions is usually the best way to go in social services.

I Had Enemies I Never Even Met

I looked forward to working at this new organization. So it felt uncomfortable when I was met with suspicion by a wary senior staff member the first day on the job. From across the room, I observed her giving me the "once over," and in a stage whisper asking her coworker, "Who's she? What's she here for?" The tone of her questions was predictive of her bullying in years to follow, and to this day I have no clue as to why she was unwelcoming, and later on, mean-spirited. This person had a disturbing habit of rolling her eyes during meetings when she disagreed with someone. It was even more disturbing that no one ever called her out on her behavior.

Over time I observed certain senior staff within this organization targeting coworkers, and I was careful to avoid their scrutiny. And so, when I was assigned to research a new grant and unintentionally discovered organization "secrets," I carefully considered the pros and cons of spilling the beans. These secrets were not illegal, but they did reflect a degree of favoritism and inequity with regard to staff compensation, and would have staged an employee revolt. After considerable thought, I took my concerns to my boss, the CEO, erroneously thinking he would appreciate the information. His response to my "revelation" was to aggressively question where I had gotten my information, and to ignore the larger issue.

Not too long after our conversation, I sensed a disturbance in my universe. At first, I was blindsided by verbal abuse from the aforementioned senior staff member and later by other key staff as well. Over time, I figured out that my targeting began when I had inadvertently entered senior management's sacred circle without permission and had questioned its integrity.

Most of the targeting I experienced was performed in front of a live audience, but there was plenty that occurred behind closed doors. My unwelcoming senior staff member's eye rolling went on overdrive when I made comments. Once, at the urging of my job coach (I went so far as to hire a job coach to advise me), I asked her how she needed my support. In reply, she grimaced as though in pain and said, "Don't open your mouth if you don't know what you're talking about!"

This offensive comment caught me off guard. True, what I don't know could fill several New Jersey landfills, but over the years I had acquired a good bit of knowledge and experience, even writing best-selling child welfare–related books.

At the time, I was literally frozen by her appalling remark and unsure how she would interpret a challenge from me to my boss, who'd brought her into the inner circle. Instead, I swallowed my abundant pride and plowed on, asking if she had a moment to schedule a meeting to discuss a mutual project. Without hesitation she bluntly replied, "Nope—don't have the time," and turned her chair away.

Instead of challenging this bully, I continued to attempt communication through e-mail, and received no response. A few of her cohorts were vigilant in their own methods of alienating me from other staff through gossip and innuendo. I thought it puzzling that, in spite of their behaviors, I continued to receive great performance reviews.

Then, the COO assigned me a pretty straightforward project. During a follow-up operations meeting he became irate when I presented the completed project for review. Looking very much like a staged event, he literally changed the project on the spot, even when the assignment sign-off sheet was placed in front of him. He followed up by saying I hadn't done my job. On their own, the organization's director of quality management and its corporate attorney, who were at the same meeting, approached me and asked why I was held in such contempt. This had not been one of my career goals.

At the same time, another senior staffer began to limit my participation in projects I had either successfully started or to which I had been a contributor. She failed to e-mail important information or include me in essential planning meetings. Once, after weeks of ignoring my messages, she responded to my desperate e-mail asking for her needed input on a new initiative by loudly stating, "I don't care about infant mental health!" (the subject of the initiative).

Coworkers began approaching me with information about these senior staff members who were discrediting my work, and even career. When I approached my bullies, to test the waters about the credibility of their reported comments, they became sullen and literally walked away from the conversation.

Me, Myself, and Why

It became more apparent that even if I were to win the Nobel Peace Prize I wasn't going to turn the situation around by myself. So, I approached my boss, who happened to be the CEO, and asked for his help. He replied that it wasn't his business. This was not a morale boost.

A few months later, on the day I returned from my nephew's funeral, he and the COO sat me down and delivered an ultimatum. Cutting right to the chase, without acknowledging my family loss, they stated that while I was of value to the organization, I would now have to work for one of the bullies who'd been marginalizing me out of my job and discrediting me to coworkers. Feeling overpowered and demoralized, I weighed my options and handed in my resignation.

On my last work day, the COO (my boss canceled) took me out for Thai food, and at the end of the meal stated that he appreciated what I had done for the organization. He also said he knew that they hadn't always made life easy for me. Amen to that.

Postmortem

Months prior to resigning I'd begun to question my abilities and tried to make sense of something—that is, my bullying—that made no sense at all. I succumbed to all of the signs of being bullied and continued to work on my self-improvement program. My contributions to the organization continued to go unnoticed, and were even downplayed.

Like most targets, I never anticipated becoming a workplace target. I erroneously believed my work spoke for itself. And while I'd observed bullying in other social services environments, I had never encountered it personally. Looking back, I recognize that, in the past, I more or less blamed targets and sometimes viewed them as complainers, or without the necessary skills to effectively negotiate their work environments. At this new career low-point, I half-wondered if my experience was bad karma for failing to recognize the severity of this workplace problem.

Being a workplace target is humiliating and, consequently, I often suffered in silence. It was an embarrassment that someone my age, with my career experience would be so poorly regarded. A few coworkers, with whom I shared my experience, validated my perceptions because they too, had been targets at one time or another. As reported by a former employee, she knew all six people working in our organization's human resources department who were prescribed antidepressants at the same time.

Like other bullied individuals, I thought at first that I was at fault. I questioned every bullying and mobbing scenario, and worked harder to make things "better," repeatedly asking my boss if there had been any complaints about me. He would change the subject. As I mentioned earlier, I hired a job coach to tutor me on how to negotiate the work culture, as well as the explosive and passive-aggressive personalities. One of my coach's final validating, but rather depressing comments at our goodbye was, "Had you stayed at that job, you would have had to sell your soul." Whoa, that's a lot to lose.

Growing Awareness

As different coworkers disappeared during my work stint, I recognized I was not a lone target. I also learned, through my own research, that workplace bullying is real, and fairly common. I discovered that many of my coworkers had left the agency because of their own bullying experiences. Staff spoke of these individuals in hushed tones, and their contributions to the organization were minimized.

With regard to workplace bullying, a code of silence existed among the workers, even though they may have experienced or observed bullying themselves. In tough economies people keep their noses to the grindstone and want to avoid situations that might put their jobs at risk. On-the-job bullying thrives when unemployment is high and organized labor is on the decline (Cohen, 2010).

As a targeted employee, I also became disillusioned by what I perceived to be a lack of, or mixed-mission, focus by various staff members. I grew to learn that the CEO was avoidant, and picked and chose protected persons with political influence. To paraphrase former U.S. Secretary of Defense Robert Gates, failing to take a stand, not backing up staff, or being hypervigilant about not "rocking the boat" is not leadership. I was uncertain if the CEO's large salary and power position overrode a more proactive stance with regard to standing up for his more vulnerable employees.

Human Resources—a Fine Line Between Saturday Night and Sunday Morning

A natural question would be "What was the human resources department doing to address this problem?" As with most nonprofit organizations, human resources departments function to protect the employer, and employees are often stuck when working in "at-will" states. (The law is pretty clear about employers pretty much being able to let folks go without cause.)

My organization's human resources administrator demonstrated through her actions that her ambition outweighed her priorities. It appeared to drive her behaviors, and she was easily threatened by talented coworkers. Her response would be to marginalize them out of the organization.

Lessons Learned

In reflecting back to my time in Oz, I now recognize that I made some fairly erroneous assumptions that contributed to or exacerbated my bullying experience. For example:

- I assumed I would receive backup and support from my boss when I shared what I'd discovered about questionable workplace practices.

- I was naive in assuming that everyone interpreted and prioritized the organization's mission in the same way.

- I thought that negotiating with rather than challenging bullies was the best way to handle my problem.

- I made false assumptions regarding my value to the organization.

- I assumed that the flow of communication would be improved by being a transparent and communicative contributor.

- I thought that coworkers would speak up on my behalf.

- For the most part, I thought I could handle the problem alone.

- I assumed that by receiving excellent work evaluations, I was immune from workplace bullying.

There are many reasons why I stayed longer than my welcome, but as I stated earlier, like domestic violence victims, I initially thought my behavior had triggered the abuse. It didn't sink in that my bullies' behaviors were theirs to own. And, as with many victims of other forms of abuse, intermittent reward, in my case through interesting work assignments, kept me hoping that my circumstances would change.

Tasks completed under budget and within timelines, money brought in by well-written proposals or curriculums, new programs built, and training hundreds of coworkers did little to elicit appreciation from upper management. I was in good company with others whose contributions were messaged to board members as leadership accomplishments, and rewarded with huge pay increases and bonuses.

My experience also prompted me to examine my motives for continuing to work on lost causes; finally shifting an old and tired belief, that if I tried hard enough people would recognize my worth. The truth is, I still had to practice internalizing something I'd learned long ago—that other people's behaviors are not about me.

The challenge for me was to find meaning behind my bullying experience, and, following a decent period of grieving for the disappointment of my hopes, I believe I have.

A profound recognition occurred for me when it finally sank in that entitlement, power, greed, and control are addictions for bullies. So, for those of us with different social welfare intentions, we'd better get out of their way. They want it all.

Neighbors Living Worlds Apart
Bullies and Targets—Targets

Target's motto: "Wow, didn't see that one coming!"

Target—"An object of verbal attack, criticism, or ridicule."

Victim—"Beast for sacrifice; someone or something killed, destroyed, or harmed." (*Webster's New World College Dictionary*, 1999)

The Ultimate Sacrifice

Charlie was a great guy, with an engaging smile and a knack for making everyone at work feel good. Retired from the military, he had gone to work at a drug and alcohol rehabilitation center as their head counselor twenty years before, and had survived several administrative changes.

Charlie, a recovering alcoholic who put in long hours, often worried over his clients and their families. He went above and beyond to ensure they were a priority, even when it became exhausting. Charlie, not one to rest on his laurels, researched evidence-based practices and worked to get his staff up to speed on new interventions.

In his twenty-first year on the job, Charlie welcomed a new CEO, a younger man in his late thirties named Dave. Dave had served on the center's board of directors, and was well-connected throughout the community as a political campaign volunteer. As a board member, he had been instrumental in easing the former agency CEO out and bringing himself on as the new administrator. He'd pitched himself as a go-getter who could bring in money and drive legislative action. His knowledge about addiction was sorely lacking, however, and his ignorance was reflected in his failure to connect with staff and clients.

Charlie found himself at management team meetings translating addiction language to the new administrator. Overriding Charlie's good intentions,

Dave questioned Charlie's experience and knowledge in front of coworkers. At one meeting, the CEO, overcome with excitement, proposed a new addiction initiative promoted by one of his political cronies. Dave pushed to implement the program, but Charlie had already researched the intervention and knew that there was little evidence to support the practice. Dave, once again, overruled Charlie's arguments.

Charlie's military background had prepared him to deal with questionable decisions, and he resolved to give the project his best effort. But unbeknownst to him, Dave had given the project assignment to one of Charlie's subordinates, putting Charlie in the awkward position of deferring to someone he supervised.

As Charlie struggled with these challenges, he discovered that Dave was taking away, with board support, staff pensions and replacing them with a non-profit IRA contribution plan. Charlie knew that many workers, earning barely minimum wage, could not afford monthly contributions to a fund. They were relying on their pensions to support them in retirement. Charlie also discovered that, at the same time, Dave and other senior managers continued to invest in a special pension fund for employees making over six figures a year. When Charlie took his concerns to Dave, the CEO challenged Charlie's integrity, and followed up by saying, "It's a difficult decision, but I know you don't want to see the agency fail."

As time wore on, Charlie's morale dropped, his blood pressure rose, and he grew depressed. Dave rarely spent time with staff, less time with clients, and was immersed in his father's political campaign, leaving staff to clean up his mistakes. Charlie was also challenged to manage staff complaints about the newly implemented program, in addition to their concerns that human resources guidelines were not followed consistently with favored employees.

Charlie spent more and more time at the office, managing agency-wide confusion and chaos. His blood pressure became dangerously high when his boss excluded him from important management meetings, and promoted the new project coordinator above him. During this time, Charlie received little feedback from his boss. His wife, growing more concerned, made a doctor's appointment for Charlie the morning he died at his desk, trying to work out employee schedules. Heart attack, the doctor reported. Charlie's wife claimed it was a heart attack brought on by a broken heart.

The Physiological Effects of Bullying

What happens to human beings when they are bullied on the job? The physical and emotional fallout can be dramatic. For example, the brain is physiologically affected by insults and put-downs. Verbal and emotional abuse, in fact, literally harms the brain.

Magnetic Resonance Imaging scans, or MRIs, are used to image the brain's response when people experience psychological trauma. A Purdue University study using real-time experiences found that insults actually trigger neuronal pain pathways in the brain. In addition, when individuals are provided with information that excludes them from enjoyable activity with others, their brains respond similarly to trauma and pain (Namie & Namie, 2011).

Stress and Workplace Bullying

Workers experience toxic stress as a result of working in hostile work environments. In addition, intense and prolonged activation of the body's stress response system alters levels of key neurochemicals, causing an internal state that disrupts normal brain function affecting memory, concentration, learning, and emotion modulation.

Continuous activation of aroused stress states can also cause compromised immune systems and metabolic regulatory functions. Toxic stress contributes to creating or exacerbating health conditions such as hypertension, heart disease, diabetes, weight gain or loss, addictions, compromised immune systems, mental illness such as depression and anxiety, and an abundance of other physical and mental health conditions described in the stories shared within this book.

In a study by Elizabeth Blackburn published in 2004, toxic stress was discovered to interfere with cellular replication by destroying telomeres, or structures that protect DNA chromosomes. Destruction of telomeres can result in shortened life spans (Kiecolt-Glaser and Glaser, 2010).

Prolonged bullying (toxic stress) also contributes to acute stress and post-traumatic stress disorder (PTSD). The Swedish researcher Heinz Leymann demonstrated that prolonged exposure to ongoing bullying creates high arousal states and anxiety, which lead to PTSD (Leymann & Gustafsson, 1990). The effects of bullying, through chronic health conditions and hyperreactive physiological and psychological responses, last much longer than the actual experience.

Acute Stress

Acute stress occurs when individuals become terrified by an out-of-the-ordinary experience and perceive themselves, or persons close to them, to be in life-threatening danger. At the time, survival systems, responding to the real or perceived threat, become overly activated, causing intense and/or prolonged arousal responses in their brains and bodies. As a result, sensory stimulation related to the memory of the experience can trigger these survival responses for about a month following the life-threatening event.

Symptoms of acute stress include intrusive thoughts, sleep disturbances, emotionality, excessive fear and anxiety, flashbacks, and markedly changed behavior, in addition to being easily triggered into repeatedly reexperiencing the terrifying event, physically and emotionally. One on-the-job example is being blindsided with a surprising demotion. If the demotion were tied to the person's survival through fear of losing his or her livelihood, the experience would shock and terrify. Following such an experience, a person might become anxious and depressed, anticipating another startling surprise.

Post-Traumatic Stress Disorder (PTSD)

Post-traumatic stress disorder lasts beyond one month and is defined by clustered physical and emotional acute stress symptoms (described above) that emerge as a result of a real or perceived life-threatening event. Formerly traumatized targets can be triggered into panic attacks and severe anxiety as past trauma memories are triggered by their bullies. For example, ongoing verbal abuse from a boss can cause PTSD to resurface. Post-traumatic stress disorder normally requires psychotherapeutic intervention. It is a condition that takes time to repair, and often includes embedding compensating life practices.

Individuals traumatized by their work experience are often prescribed antidepressants, sleep aids, and anti-anxiety medication. Their psychic wounds can leave lasting scars that prevent them from trusting subsequent employers and experiencing a spontaneous quality of life.

Should targets attempt to bring legal action against their perpetrators, it is usually at their own cost. If the case is dismissed or ruled in favor of the bad guys, they have an additional challenge, as they once again experience victimization; only this time by the legal system. It's back to therapy.

Formerly bullied targets have also been permanently disabled by their abuse, and for physical or mental health reasons, are unable to return to work. Data from Sweden (Leymann & Gustafsson, 1996) estimate that approximately 15 percent of all suicides in Sweden could be attributed to workplace bullying. Other researchers have validated that almost half of the victims in their surveys contemplated suicide (Davenport et al., 2005).

Impact of Workplace Bullying
Anxiety
Diminished quality of life
Depression and anger
Low morale
Isolation
Shame
Feelings of worthlessness
Humiliation and guilt
Irrational thinking and paranoia
Impaired relationships
Sleep disorders
Loss of purposeful work
Poor job performance
Hypertension
Hypervigilance
Panic attacks
Loss of income
Medication management
Addiction

Toxic stress

Suicidal ideation

Loss of confidence

Heart disease

Digestive problems

Psychologically unsafe

Prolonged or higher incidences of chronic health conditions

Degrees—Analogous to Those for Burns—of Target Impairment as a Result of Workplace Bullying

First degree: Targets identify their abuse, suffer moderate impairment, and are supported through the experience to move forward at their workplace, or have found work elsewhere.

Second degree: Targets are unable to identify and receive support for their abuse immediately, and as a result, experience temporary or prolonged mental and/or physical impairment, with difficulty reentering the workforce.

Third degree: Targets are unable to reenter the workforce due to mental and/or physical impairment. Rehabilitation is not possible without a prolonged recovery and assisted specialized support through medication management and/or psychotherapy. (Davenport et al., 2005)

A Target's Past Can Get in the Way

Those working in social services can make especially ripe targets when their past traumas contribute to their stress. For example, the field of social services often attracts individuals who have trauma histories. They choose their vocation in order to give their former suffering meaning. These folks, at a core level, understand clients. Yet, unless repaired over time, their coping mechanisms formed earlier as a result of trauma, open the door to blurring their personal boundaries. Because of their inability to set firm emotional boundaries, formerly traumatized workers often have a problem saying "no" and/or standing up for themselves. In these instances, these workers can find themselves between a rock and a hard place, when bullies are verbally abusive, and bosses continue to raise performance bars.

In addition, formerly traumatized social services workers may be extra empathic, and will often make excuses for their bully's behaviors. They may believe that by not confronting their bullies, the problem will go away by itself. Boundaries become further blurred when they transfer their empathy onto coworkers and bosses as well as those bullying them. Their practiced behaviors and beliefs, rooted in childhood, prompt them to naturally absorb others' bad behavior. And, once in the soup, targets have a difficult time objectively assessing their situations. Working becomes an extension of their former trauma (Brohl, 2005).

With the (conscious or unconscious) determination of righting past trauma suffering, workers often overly commit to work, literally becoming addicted to it. But working long hours is exhausting and can prompt the breakdown of one's coping defenses. Consequently, exhausted workers are more likely to become open books when they express their emotions; bullies can perceive this as "weakness" and go in for the kill. For example, an overwhelmed employee, recently passed over for a promotion, was sitting in his cubicle when an office bully entered. She stated she knew he had not gotten the job, and, rubbing salt in the wound asked whether he "was really ready to assume the responsibility." Her target simply shrugged.

Adding Insult to Injury

In the world of workplace bullying, the law rules out and addresses issues that have to do with who gets harmed by whom when it comes to bullying. According to the 2007 Workplace Bullying Institute and Zogby International (WBI-Zogby) Polling Survey, 37 percent of American adults said they had been bullied on the job. Most of it was legal. The laws do not protect against meanness, unless those bringing the complaint fall under protected abused classes that can sue under civil rights laws. Unfortunately, the laws protect only about 20 percent of bullied workers.

Since suing their employers is not often an option, targets are once again on the short end of the stick when it comes to resolving their situations. Most targets quit their jobs, at a tremendous cost to the workforce. The WBI-Zogby survey estimated that 54 million employees are bullied and 24 percent of bullied targets are fired, while 13 percent transfer to another part of the organization. Females were more likely to quit than men. An encouraging 23 percent of bullies are punished. But a rather disturbing 62 percent of employers who are made aware of bullying either escalate targets' problems or don't do anything about them. Employers help only about one-third of the time.

The Social Service Target—A Self-Preservation Society of One

"A broken soul stares from a pair of watering eyes / Uncertain emotions force an uncertain smile." ("Uncertain Smile," *The Nicely*)

At first blush it would appear that targets are just too nice; and it's true, Boy Scouts and Girl Scouts have nothing over workplace targets. Targets share the following traits:

Loyalty

Openness and honesty

Commitment to doing a job well

Transparency

Optimism

Cooperation

Mission focus

These are great qualities, but at the same time, they place employees at higher risk of being bullied on the job.

Targets are not saints, but they are people who tend to believe problems will naturally sort themselves out. They also, rather magically, believe they will be recognized for their work contributions. For all their strengths, targets are naive when it comes to reading others' intentions and understanding that not everyone looks at the world through the same colored lenses. Because they approach work with a cooperative attitude, they assume others will do the same. Their attitudes are an asset in the world of social services.

While understanding client-related job risks, targets normally assume that working within their own helping-profession workplace culture is safe. In a target's mind, if the cause is right, and people share the same mission, coworkers would not psychologically abuse one another. It doesn't make sense to someone with sincere and altruistic intentions. When it occurs, it can turn a target's worldview upside down and highlights the fact that not everyone within the same organization agrees on the same mission.

In addition, by the time a person has made the decision to pursue a social advocacy career, he or she understands that, generally, it doesn't pay much. And, in fact, most new workers are in the dark about how much money administrators can actually earn, or the power they can wield. There is a larger assumption by most frontline workers that bosses are underpaid and at least looking out for their own employees' interest. This is where their trusting nature and naiveté work against them. Although many employers are mindful of staff compensation, straddling the fine line of rationalizing their personal income and endorsing pay raises gets tricky in tough economies.

Who Are Targets?

In addition to their rather optimistic outlook on life, targets also bring their own personalities and skill sets to the workplace. These personality traits can further prompt bullying behavior.

Nonconforming Employees

Nonconforming individuals bring much in the way of creativity and innovation to their social services organizations. Yet, when fear becomes the only work incentive, they stick out like a sore thumb because they simply won't respond. Nonconformists do not respond well to rigid work structures, or fear-based cultures.

People get labeled as nonconformists when they don't fit in with cultural norms in the workplace, and the criteria can be pretty arbitrary and fickle. For example, if the majority of people in the office eat lunch together while one person chooses to eat alone, guess who's labeled a nonconformist?

Social services organizations may appear, on the surface, to be more accepting and kind toward their own. In reality, however, many can be rigid and blameful social structures. Social services is a fairly conforming environment, and if some administrators are threatened by nonconformers, they'll get rid of them. Remember, bullies are drawn to people like themselves (their own reflections), often at the exclusion of others. And, as stated earlier, bullies feel threatened by someone "different."

Nonconformists characteristically assume that other people appreciate them for what they can bring to the table, as they mostly appreciate others. Unfortunately, nonconformists are folks who unknowingly walk into a hornet's nest, because they're not aware of "sacred circle" decision-making. And there's the rub—their good intentions are often misunderstood. By contrast, bullies don't have the best of intentions. And their tendency is to project their own intentions onto others. Consequently, nonconformists are often labeled troublemakers when they innocently ask, "Hey, what's this invoice for?" or "I thought you said you were getting rid of pensions, but I see here you all are signed up."

Overly Qualified Employees

In times of economic recession, many social services organizations have had to cut personnel in order to stay afloat, leaving highly qualified and experienced social services professionals searching for new work. Administrators are able, in tough economies, to hire overly qualified people for positions where they once struggled to find individuals with marginal qualifications.

However, when bosses hire people with more experience and knowledge, it can be a setup for these new folks to become targets. Bullies find them threatening, especially when the bullies, themselves, have been promoted through the "Peter Principle" (elevated to higher positions beyond their skill sets). Threatened, they'll work to identify flaws in new hires.

Overqualified new workers struggle to work with coworkers who might also label them "entitled," and/or spread erroneous rumors about them. Workplace bullies may also use their targets' minor mistakes to pick them apart in front of others.

Assertive Employees

Some folks are naturally comfortable speaking up when they see a problem, and will resist backing down when challenged. They open themselves up to being targeted. Assertive people in social services walk a fine between being politically correct, and putting a voice to what everyone else has been thinking. Bullies abhor a verbal challenge from targets, whom they consider inferior. Consequently, these targeted individuals are not present at board of directors meetings. And on rare occasions, when targets speak up within politically charged environments, bullies may outwardly laugh alongside their targets, but proceed to shred them when the right moment presents itself.

"Misplaced" Employees

When organizations are scrambling to meet timelines and rotating legislative agendas, or when administrators and managers lack knowledge about open positions, social service professionals can be placed in the wrong jobs for their skill sets. When this occurs, the employee and supervisor often struggle to figure out how to make the match work. Job placement is a huge workplace consideration. If supervisors are not prepared to coach someone to competency, or are otherwise unskilled at transferring their supervisee away from or to another position within the organization, bullying can emerge.

The employee will quickly lose confidence as the supervisor continues to point and blame without designing and documenting a compassionate plan of action.

When Employees Are Falsely Branded with a Mental Health Diagnosis

Bullies use gossip as assault weapons. Skilled bullies will seamlessly drop in pieces of gossip when speaking to their supervisors. For example, one reported bully has a habit of dropping in an "after-message" at the end of a conversation. "Chris seems to struggle with her emotions, and it presents a problem on the project. I think she's emotionally fragile (eye roll), but best leave that one lie, if you know what I mean" (another eye roll).

Within mental health organizations, targets are more often given extremely negative personality-disorder diagnoses by their bullies. The one most often used is the diagnosis of borderline personality disorder, normally a diagnosis that takes lengthy evaluation, but one that has been overworked by bullies. Someone who is authentically diagnosed with this disorder has a history of unstable behavior and relationships. When frustrated targets eventually erupt in anger or cry on the job owing to yet another humiliation by their bullies, their perpetrators are quick to validate their assertions with such comments as "I told you this one is borderline."

Neighbors Living Worlds Apart

Targets and bullies work in parallel universes. For example, targets will usually attempt to cooperate, while bullies cooperate when it suits their needs. Targets cooperate because they think it contributes to a less stressful work environment.

Bullies don't care about cooperating unless it serves their purposes, and they are more inclined to throw targets off balance by being inconsistent and unpredictable.

Targets are loyal; bullies identify those "worthy" of their loyalty. One reported agency director routinely curries favor with her boss, but has thrown her coworkers under the bus on several occasions (after which she'll say to her bruised colleague, "I thought I was supporting you. I had no idea you would be affected. I feel so guilty.").

Targets are probably too transparent about their feelings for their own good. One very successful social welfare advocate stated that her downfall at her former social services agency was sharing one frustrated moment with a bully. She allowed her emotions to get the better of her. In retrospect, she acknowledges that her bully was looking for the right time to steal her work, and he used that one instance to bounce back to her that she didn't need any more job pressure. This "bounce back" tactic is often used by workplace bullies.

Targets often pride themselves on being open and honest, which is not exactly the best way to bypass workplace bullying. One woman remarked that she became concerned that two agency V.P.s were drinking heavily after-hours with staff. She felt that their behaviors sent the wrong signals about propriety, and didn't paint senior managers in the best light. She took her concerns to her boss, and within days began to experience icing out by management. Eventually, their behaviors created enough stress to push her to quit her job.

Social welfare targets are generally optimistic. "Tomorrow is another day" could be their mantra. Optimism is a terrific resiliency characteristic but doesn't help when targets are getting bullied. Optimism promotes "magical thinking." "Wake up and smell the coffee!" would be a better mantra.

When targets allow their thoughts to follow the yellow brick road of magical thinking their abuse continues. Confronting the bully gets sidelined because a target would rather imagine only good intentions coming from a bully. A target is likely to think, "Cynthia will eventually see me as the dedicated contributor I am." Wrong. Cynthia will rely on the fact that her target plays fair. By comparison, bullies justify themselves by thinking that "all's fair in love and war."

"Didn't See That One Coming" or "How Did I Get Here?"

Let's look at how bullying plays out for the target. In general, it normally follows a sequence of events:

1. An employee is targeted.

2. The normally unaware target becomes engaged in conflict with the bully, and may not know a problem exists until she gets wind of gossip, or is passed over for a promotion.

3. Bullying escalates.

4. The target experiences the fallout from the abuse, meaning hypertension, isolation, psychological estrangement, sleep disorders, etc.

5. The target is labeled a problem.

6. The target considers his or her options and moves forward to resolve the problem.

1. Targeted

Workers are targeted for any number of reasons, many already described. Bullies and targets don't need to have been recently introduced. In fact, they may have gotten along for a time, until a bully identifies the colleague as a threat or in some way inferior. The bully may have been promoted or otherwise gained an upper hand with regard to a power differential between him/herself and the target.

Mark and Lawrence

Longtime coworkers, Mark became a favorite for promotion. Lawrence had encouraged and supported Mark through some very difficult times, and was pleased for his friend.

However, when Mark received his promotion and became a senior manager, things changed. He distanced himself from Lawrence. As he engaged further with fellow managers, he felt like he'd been invited into the "sacred circle." Lawrence seldom heard from his old friend unless Mark needed help from Lawrence.

In the meantime, other senior managers had identified Lawrence as a weak employee who lacked confidence to do the job. Lawrence, for his part, was a naturally quiet person, but his quiet strength was misinterpreted by senior-level bullies.

The relationship turned south when Mark assumed greater authority. And when Lawrence was put on the short list for employee cuts, Mark felt that if he advocated for Lawrence's job, he might be perceived as playing favorites. When the ax finally fell, Lawrence sought out Mark's support, but Mark ignored his messages.

During the initial targeting phase, bullies meet or already know their targets and begin to identify them as a problem. Described earlier, their assumptions have more to do with a bully's transference and projection issues. In addition, ego and ambition figure into the picture. As bullies size up their victims, they may ask themselves:

- How does this person hold me back from what I want?

- How can this person's job threaten my career and income?

- How can I use this person's vulnerability to get what I want?

- How do I diminish this person in front of others to make myself look better?

- How do I use this person to get ahead?

- How could this person block my ambition?

- How can I get this person's job?

- How do I assert or communicate my superiority to this person?

2. Engagement and Conflict

Targets will make attempts to work with their bullies. Though they've already been identified and targeted, most of the time they have no clue. A minor conflict can prompt their abuse, and may range from the target's threatening skill sets to an on-the-job mistake that could portray a bully in a bad light. It can even be a situation where the target has run across some incriminating information about the bully or the organization and has brought it to management's attention.

3. Escalation

The bully makes the first move. One tactic is to throw the target under the bus by making a pejorative comment, or withdrawing suddenly from a project that supports the target's work.

The target is normally stunned, but probably rationalizes that the bully was having a bad day. The target probably shrugs off the bully's aggressive behavior. Within a few weeks, the bully amps it up by "calling the target out" in front of coworkers, or diminishing the target behind his or her back. The bully's comments are meant to humiliate the target and make the target look bad to bosses. Again, the target approaches the problem by thinking that the best way to address any issues is to go right to the bully and ask if there is a problem. The bully ignores or minimizes the target's concerns, but continues to escalate the behavior by removing the target from projects, or withdrawing support, and even blocks the target's efforts to complete work assignments.

4. Fallout

Unless their egos are superbly intact, targets usually respond to their treatment by first blaming themselves. Their further attempts to contact and to coordinate effective communication are sidelined or blocked. As a result, targets begin to experience isolation and disconnect at work, otherwise known as psychological estrangement. They will struggle to grasp their situation, and question whether their concerns are based in reality. They begin to consider taking their problem to human resources or a higher authority. Often, the negatives outweigh the positives, because bullies probably have a direct communication line to the top—or are the top. When one target reached out to her boss, the conversation went something like this:

Target, after explaining her situation to her boss: "I am at a loss as to where to go from here. I'm coming to you for help. I would really appreciate any assistance you might provide in this matter."

Boss: "I am not interested in being in the middle, although I am definitely interested in anything that moves the process in a positive direction."

In other words, "Huh?"

After another few months, as the bully continues to roll merrily along, the target reaches out again to her boss.

Boss: "Perhaps I am oversensitive, but it does seem that you remain suspicious about Shelly's (the bully) motives for a variety of actions.

"I know you react to the evidence around you, and I do not question that . . . I do see that maintaining your vigilance against expected negative behavior from Shelly can sap your own vibrant energy, and that is a waste."

In frustration the target responds.

Target: "Please know my strength/energies are not being sapped by being hyper-vigilant with Shelly. I am more wary, not hypervigilant. I would be foolish to assume her behavior will miraculously change, and naive to think that anyone would apologize."

In this instance, the target's boss is completely sidestepping the issue and not admitting any wrongdoing on the part of Shelly. The target's boss is protecting herself, and also failing to acknowledge that Shelly is being a pill. She is not acknowledging, or taking any responsibility for investigating, the situation.

When bullying is reported, human resources departments often find themselves caught between listening politely to the target, and looking out for the organization's best interests. Many human resources directors have left their jobs because their own professional integrity conflicted with their employers' wishes.

5. Labeled as a Troublemaker, or the Village Idiot

Targets begin to suffer emotionally and physically. They often lose sleep trying to figure something out that doesn't make sense. As their frustration and exhaustion grow, often along with a health problem, they may risk losing their professional credibility by reacting impulsively to their abuse. Given the right triggers, targets risk behaving impulsively and doing something that will be used against them.

Having gotten their targets to this place of frustration and anger, bullies relish the opportunity to point out the targets' flaws. They delight in spreading rumors that have to do with the targets' "apparent" inability to control themselves at work. Coworkers may now view the target with skepticism, and wonder if the target's reported bullying experiences have been exaggerated.

Every facet of a target's life is affected by workplace bullying. In other words, targets become unbalanced with regard to their emotional, physical, spiritual, relaxation, work, relationship, and family markers that reflect their quality of life. As a result, unsettling feelings and emotions can take hold. Ongoing stress caused by surprise attacks by their perpetrators creates anxiety and paranoia. Yet their paranoia is situational and is more often based in reality.

In addition, targets struggle to balance life outside of work. Mentally figuring out how to fix the problem becomes an ongoing obsession for them. Obsessed with righting their situations, this distraction can become intrusive in everyday life, as well as during family celebrations and vacations. Frustration and low morale play a part in a target's emotions; and often, the fallout from these feelings occurs in the target's own home. Family members have been vicarious victims of workplace bullying, when the rudeness of bullies has a ripple effect beyond the office. A study at Baylor University found that working with horrible coworkers can generate stress for the target's family as well, including bleeding stress into the target's partner's workplace (Yu, 2012). This tension can erode normal routines, as targets and their partners turn to sleep as an escape or even worse, to addictions. In addition, targets and their mates have often taken their stress to the mall, finding temporary relief in shopping, and as a result, find themselves in debt.

Grasping that on-the-job bullying is betrayal causes an array of conflicting feelings. Bullies betray their targets through social structures, as well as their own behaviors. Targets normally want to trust coworkers, but when betrayal enters the picture, it's devastating and disheartening. The very nature of their social advocacy is to support or aid in solving problems, and the fact that they cannot fix their own is demoralizing.

Shame becomes part of their emotional malaise as well, because targets are often identified as problem children, and separated from the herd. "Shame on you for being who you are" is the mob's message. Shame may feed into old feelings of being the kid not picked for the team, or the adolescent who enjoyed math too much. Taken from an old Alcoholics Anonymous adage, "stinking thinking" can rear its ugly head and feed into self-talk that has to do with not being good enough.

Targets often experience situational depression because they are unable to control their bullying. Consequently, depression turns into self-doubt, which takes on a life of its own. Distorted thinking becomes part of the mix by becoming patterned. Some examples include:

• No one else seems to be troubled by my boss's behavior. It's probably something I did.

- If I tried another angle maybe the bully might understand where I'm coming from.

- Perhaps if I really think about how they must be feeling, I'll understand things a little better and make some changes.

- It's not about them; it's about how I handle myself with them.

- It's my own fault. I must have done something to tick her off.

- I guess I deserved what they dished out.

- I'm probably not very good at getting along with people.

- Maybe they're right. I haven't been listening.

- If my boss doesn't have confidence in me, I probably don't deserve this job.

- How can I twist myself into someone they respect?

- I wonder when I'll be replaced, fired, or laid off?

Social service clients also suffer a betrayal when targets, owing to stress, fail to develop treatment plans or turn in court reports. And clients suffer when their case managers quit because of workplace bullying. Clients, with their own trust issues, are back to square one when they're forced to work with new case managers, not to mention that important timelines affecting their court deadlines are postponed.

6. Considering Options, Taking Action, and Moving Forward

Targets will generally continue to suffer in silence until their work environment becomes toxic. They finally reach a precipice where they need to consider their professional options. Depending on their circumstances, a smooth transition to another social service function may quickly solve the problem. More likely, targets will patiently work at leaving with references intact. At the other end of the spectrum, they might impulsively quit, appearing to others as having taken out-of-the-blue and graceless action. An even worse case scenario is leaving as a result of a debilitating mental or physical condition that impacts their ability to work again.

At this juncture, targets have identified and now move to address the problem, while not feeling at the top of their game. Work shapes lives, and gives them meaning. The field of social services is especially meaningful to people who dedicate themselves to doing good works.

When targets leave their jobs because of bullying, they not only feel that their professional lives have stalled, but also that what they've done on behalf of their clients has gone unrecognized. Run off by bullies at work, it's easy to become depressed and angry. One target stated, "My experience has left a permanent scar."

In addition, targets' social life is often disrupted because coworker friends have usually become part of their social network and support system. Targets grieve not only the loss of their meaningful work, but the loss of relationships as well.

Depending on how targets go about leaving their jobs, new work will be found either sooner or later. For example, if the departure is acrimonious, obtaining good references from former employers, in spite of human resources regulations, can be a slippery slope. If the departure has been smooth, meaning targets complied with workplace departure guidelines and didn't alienate persons in power, positive work references may follow. It takes self-control for targets to leave their jobs with their dignity and references intact.

In addition, planning for one's departure takes patience, especially when leaving under duress, and/or when there is a slowed job market. Many professionals choose demotions and/or large pay cuts in order to leave behind the toxic stress.

Letting Go of a Dream

Individuals targeted at work not only grieve the disappointment of their professional desires, they also experience a larger sadness that has to do with the reasons they entered social services to begin with. Targets more often view their work as a "calling" rather than a job. It feels good to be of service to others. Feelings of hopelessness and sadness balloon when targets are denied or barred from following their dreams. During these moments they need to recognize there are other dreams waiting to be uncovered.

In addition, in difficult economic times, targets carry more of the burden to prove their bullies wrong, just as those groups now protected by law had to. Often disabled by labels and hostile actions, targets are required to rescue their own reputations, and pull their professional lives back together.

Although tolerating abuse and bending to accommodate a bullying workplace is always an option, it is not the best recipe for keeping one's integrity and physical or mental condition together. To quote Nelson Mandela's 1994 inaugural address as the new president of South Africa, "There is nothing enlightening about shrinking so that other people won't feel unsure around you."

Bullies have no right to harm, or drive others from their jobs. They are narcissistically impaired and pathologically insensitive, lacking insight about how their own behaviors work to destroy people's physical and psychological well-being. Ironically, once their targets have been driven from the workplace, bullies forget, and even deny, any wrongdoing. "Out of sight, out of mind" means it never happened.

A cruel irony occurs when social services work environments harm their own while professing that their mission is to improve the lives of others. There is no justification for what occurs when bullying takes hold in the social services workplace. No justification at all.

6

The Fickle Value of Friendship: How Bystanders Function in the Workplace

Bystander motto: "Better them than me."

Bystander—"A person who stands near, but does not participate." (*Webster's New World College Dictionary*, 1999)

Incorporating Bystanders into the Bullying Scenario

Bystanders may not start out participating in workplace bullying, but as is often the case, they become involved, not only as observers, but as vicarious bullies as well. The following story illustrates how bystanders get drawn in.

The Project

Allison, Harvey, Bruce, and Deb were given a project assignment, to research and write a feasibility study on elder care for their child-safety organization. Mid-level managers, they began the project with little direction from their boss, the CEO. Instead, per his usual approach to large projects, he gave an ambiguous directive. When group members asked the purpose of the study, their boss replied that he wanted to look at other revenue streams for the organization, even though the agency's mission clearly spelled out something different.

Group members met, and Deb, by virtue of her longtime relationship with the boss, assumed she would take the lead on the project. The boss, however, chose the newest hire, Bruce, to take the lead. Bruce followed up by scheduling their first meeting to develop an operational plan. Deb came late, and spent the entire time texting and answering her phone. During the last ten minutes of the meeting, Bruce struggled to get the group to agree on their short-term goals, while Deb struggled to monopolize the conversation.

Bruce sent out a request for agenda topics for the next meeting, and heard from everyone except Deb. Between meetings, he'd seen her pop into Harvey and Allison's offices, but thought nothing of it until all project members, except Bruce, arrived late. Bruce began to introduce the agenda, when Deb piped up that she had recently been given another assignment that was taking up her time. Unfortunately it precluded her continuing to work on the study. As if on cue, Harvey and Allison interjected that they, too, were overwhelmed, and unable to continue. Bruce was left to complete the entire feasibility study alone. When he took this newest challenge to his boss, the CEO just shrugged.

In this scenario, Allison and Harvey allowed themselves to be drawn in by Deb, the bully. The situation became part of a group dynamic where everyone participated in "icing" Bruce out, and leaving him alone to handle the work. Deb was jealous that he'd been picked to be the study's point person. In addition, she'd asked herself, "What if Bruce is more capable?" She would risk losing her power differential with Bruce.

She encouraged Harvey's complaints about Bruce's lack of experience at their organization. He felt that Bruce needed to earn his dues before being given such a high-level assignment. Allison was bothered by their conspiracy, but felt more loyalty to Deb and Harvey because they'd worked together longer.

The boss had an ulterior motive, to see how Bruce could demonstrate leadership. But he translated Deb's behavior, and the abdication by the other two, as their lack of confidence in Bruce's ability to lead. Had he investigated a bit more, he would not have made false assumptions.

As it happened, Bruce had no chance out of the starting gate. Deb was clearly the most aggressive of the crew, and used her power position to leave Bruce hanging, along with the impression that he was inept. Allison and Harvey, spearheaded by Deb, became accomplices. Allison could have remained a bystander by not participating in Deb and Harvey's behaviors, but, sadly, was drawn into the abuse. Bruce never knew what hit him.

The Role of Bystanders in Workplace Bullying

A picture pops into mind when bullying bystanders are brought into the mix. The imagined scene includes a large animal (bully) lunging at a kitten (the target), while the townsfolk watch in horror. They freeze and are incapable of saving the kitten. They simply cannot rescue the kitten, yet believe someone else will.

This image may contribute to the general consensus that bystanders play no role in workplace bullying. Bystanders have been given the unspoken nod to just stand by and do nothing when they witness bullying. But their passiveness encourages the abuse.

In a study on workplace bullying (Fisher-Blando, 2011), 75 percent of study participants reported they witnessed mistreatment of coworkers at some point during their careers. Most did nothing to report the problem or intervene on behalf of the target. Bystanders have been quick to provide excuses such as:

- "It happened so fast, I didn't understand what was going on."

- "I felt somehow like things were going in slow motion and felt frozen to challenge the bully."

- "I don't know what workplace bullying is because it seems like it's normal here."

- "I know the guy didn't deserve the bullying, but honestly, I think he's an idiot."

- "My friend's not a bully. The person asked for it. It's not my friend's fault."

- "Someone will report this, but I'm not going to."

- "I don't really care what goes on here. I'm just putting in my time. All I want is my paycheck."

- "I don't owe anyone anything."

- "The woman's a loser and deserved what she got."

- "I could be the next target if I challenge the boss on this."

- "I hate to admit this, but I felt relieved that she was gone, even though she didn't deserve her abuse."

According to social psychologists, other reasons that explain bystander behavior include:

1. Bystanders create their own exaggerated negative retaliation projections should they challenge bullies, or report workplace bullying. For example, they fear for their jobs, or becoming the next person targeted. They also fear being associated with the perceived "weaker" target, and/or have learned that speaking up won't get them ahead.

2. Bystanders take the path of least resistance. It's just easier. In addition, they easily rationalize that there is more to be gained by not speaking up or defending

the target. "Keep your head down and go about your own business" is their motto.

3. Bystanders use targets as scapegoats when things go wrong. They will turn on people who might have in the past spoken on their behalf. When things go south in the workplace, these bystanders become vicarious bullies by pointing their finger back to targets, who may even be part of their social circle. Targets are convenient persons to blame because they are perceived as the weakest links within the system.

4. Bystanders normally want to affiliate with the most powerful. It keeps them feeling safe, and adds to self-perceptions that they are winners. Given their fickle nature, bystanders are not averse to moving their loyalty from one person to another quickly when politics change in the workplace.

5. Bystanders identify vicariously with bullies by allowing them to carry out their personal projections. They may even experience pleasure in witnessing others in distress. For example, if targets appear to have easier lives by virtue of their accomplishments, education, or economic circumstances, bystanders may enjoy observing their coworkers' psychological pain. Bystanders may think that newly departed targets have impeded their own professional opportunities, and rationalize, "One person's lemon is another person's lemonade."

6. Some bystanders regard reasonable and civilized target responses to bullying as weakness rather than a sign of maturity. In addition, they may have been groomed by bullies to believe that targets deserve their abuse.

7. Bystanders may be ignorant about workplace bullying, and assume that because their work's purpose is to help others, workplace bullying isn't possible. When it happens, they simply don't know what to do. They may also lack the emotional intelligence to understand the ramifications of workplace bullying. In addition, they may not recognize the more subtle behaviors associated with bullying, nor realize they share in responsibility to stop it. Or, they might not recognize target behaviors, and assume targets are not affected.

Many bystanders still share a view that targets are the sole owners of their abuse. American workplace culture was structured on the belief that "pulling oneself up by the bootstraps" is the best way to handle problems. In other words, when people flounder, it's because they are lacking.

In addition, hardworking bullied targets may be appreciated for what they bring to work, but are also threatening to those who believe that being too dedicated is dangerous. In a work environment where inertia has taken hold, a "go-getter" is a threat to antiquated work practices and workers who've grown lazy.

Passive bystanders also believe that the workplace is not a place to build relationships, and that friendships at work are transitory. They question why they would be obligated to defend a coworker.

When bullying is embedded in the social structure of an organization, bystanders may view bullying as normal and go about their business apathetic about the problem. As part of the norm, bullies have more than likely gone through the department and subtly cautioned bystanders, through rumor, against helping the target. Bullies are good at manipulating people's perceptions with intent to engender a negative view of the target. Sometimes bullies even use implied threats that pertain to reorganizing or disciplining people who intercede on behalf of the target.

When fear drives workers, they will be afraid to speak up or take action. For example, workers hesitate to cross an aggressor known for being devious and mean-spirited. In addition, if some employees are marginal at their work, they are not likely to expose their vulnerability by speaking on behalf of someone else. Finally, some people are just better at deferring to and currying favor with bullies.

Bystander Effect (Genovese Syndrome)

The bystander effect is a social psychological phenomenon that occurs when people fail to assist victims in emergency situations while others are present. The greater the number of bystanders, the less likely they will help the victim. Named for Kitty Genovese, murdered in 1964, researchers launched a series of experiments that resulted in one of the strongest and most replicable effects in social psychology. During an emergency, bystanders monitor the reactions of other people to see if others intervene. Pluralistic ignorance occurs when everyone is monitoring bystander reactions while the victim is ignored. Known as diffusion of responsibility, bystanders assume someone else is going to help a victim (Darley & Latane, 1968).

While the bystander effect was first based on violent acts toward victims, it could also be applied to workplace bullying, where bystanders check to see how someone else will address the problem. For example, at a large meeting, a senior manager rolls his eyes when his target speaks. Coworkers observe the behavior, and look to see how others react. Consequently, no one challenges the bullying. In another situation, an older worker is chastised by the boss in front of a small circle of coworkers. She is clearly distraught, but colleagues, thinking someone else will reach out to her, ignore her.

The Bystander's Role in Addressing and Stopping Workplace Bullying

Bystanders help to continue bullying in social services when they fail to act on behalf of targets. They contribute to further suffering. Employers can begin to identify and address the problem by using a variety of approaches that include:

1. Educating all workers to recognize bullying behaviors

2. Educating the workforce that silence legitimizes bullying

3. Educating everyone about the bystander's role, and how to challenge bullies while still protecting themselves (Omari, 2010).

Bystanders must grasp that workplace bullying creates a fear-based environment that is psychologically unsafe. For instance, if one works at a domestic-violence program and the boss is psychologically abusive to staff, it replicates the same type of hostile culture they are working to address and eliminate. Workers are challenged to relate to abused victims, and at the same time, to deal with their own abuse.

Taking Action

In the ideal world, there wouldn't be workplace bullying—especially in social services organizations. If bullying were to occur, bystanders would take action. But in the current work environment, bystanders are frequently drawn in because they work in a dysfunctional culture that employs, encourages, and perpetuates the problem. Sticking up for a coworker takes some courage, but it does leave one's integrity and character intact. And besides, it's the right thing to do. Here's what you can do if you witness bullying in your workplace:

- Step in immediately to stop the bullying. Using a clear, firm voice, let the bully know the behavior is wrong. If that's not possible, leave the room and let someone in a position of authority know. Also, let bullies know their behavior isn't funny, or the least attractive.

- Do not join bullies in their abusive behaviors. Joining them makes you just one more bully.

- Do not participate in, or pass along unkind rumors started by workplace bullies. Rumors gain momentum in the workplace.

- Refrain from gossiping about targets in front of known bullies, who will use the information against their victims.

- Never put a colleague in danger by keeping secrets that could adversely impact their job safety, or publicly humiliate them. For example, if you know someone is being "iced out" of important meetings, let the person know, and speak up on his/her behalf.

- Support and sympathize with targets. Victims need to know they're not alone; it lessens their tendency to isolate themselves from coworkers. Demonstrate your support by reassuring targets that they are not to blame for the abuse.

- Do not allow bullies to demonstrate their support for you by bullying others. Allowing their behaviors makes you a bully as well.

- Distract the bully from continuing to abuse the target. Change the subject, or interject a joke to lighten the situation. Afterward, tell the bully that the behaviors weren't appropriate.

- Report bullying incidents, and let people know you don't feel psychologically safe working within an organization that allows bullying to continue. Be specific.

- There is power in numbers. Check around to see if others notice workplace bullying, and ask them if they would be willing to file a group complaint. It will have impact.

In the end, bullies at work must be stopped! Through education and workplace support, bystanders have an opportunity to make a huge contribution in addressing the problem. They are part of the larger solution for changing the ways in which social services organizations hurt their own.

A Need and Good Intentions:
A Brief History of Social Services
in the United States

Question: What does the history of social services work have to do with workplace bullying?

Answer: Understanding social services history promotes greater awareness about its impact on current-day policies, social structures, and practice that contribute to workplace bullying.

Old English Poor Laws and Their Carryover to Present-Day Social Services

Before the American Revolution, systems of care for children, the mentally ill, and the poor were pretty much established by the English in North America. These systems were guided by roughly five hundred years of English Poor Laws that drove perceptions of who was "worthy" of public aid, and can also be traced back to the Poor Law of 1601. The goal of the Poor Law of 1601 was to reduce the costs of poor relief (Mandelker, 1956).

These perspectives carried an assumption that individuals came by their conditions through their own fault. Individuals were scrutinized regarding their fitness to receive relief assistance, and strict rules applied to how they should behave as a result of the help given.

The English influence also saw the value of having poor people in society who could do the more unpleasant tasks that needed to be done. And, because of the societal view that those in need were responsible for their misfortunes, they should be given only the bare minimum of assistance. It was also feared by those in power that providing people with opportunities greater than their immediate need would cause them to rise up and overpower their "betters."

Far from ideal, the English Poor Laws paved the way in bringing the problems of the poor to light, and moving them from beneath the weight of feudal systems.

Compared with today's standards, the English Poor Laws appear primitive, but they served a dual purpose of demonstrating compassion and offering protection to those less fortunate.

Basic principles were interwoven into providing aid through these laws, and created many present-day social welfare policies and social structures. They include:

1. Poverty is a human failing, and not a consequence of economic or societal changes.

2. Everyone able to work must work. It is imperative to keep the poor working when they are able, in order to meet the need for individuals to perform low-paying and unpleasant tasks. If these people refuse there will be severe public humiliation and punishment.

3. There is an ongoing search for ways to cut costs of providing relief (help) to the poor.

4. Change is inevitable in helping the poor, because previous efforts will soon be the subject of reform and criticized as insufficient.

5. Wages and freedom of poor people who do work must be tightly regulated and if necessary, coercion must be employed to keep them working at low wages. Any refusal on the part of the employer or worker will be punished, with greater punishment dealt to the worker.

6. The survival of the nonworking poor transitioned from feudal systems and the church to civil authority, and is largely a local public responsibility (Quigley, 1996).

The English Poor Laws set the stage for continuous social welfare reform that bled into the twenty-first century. Still, today, ongoing change dominates social service systems. Also, the issue of who is worthy of help remains a constant point of discussion among social welfare advocates and political pundits.

In addition, the Old English Poor Laws judged people for how they received help or assistance. If they were perceived to be resistant, or unable to bounce back from their economic or physical challenges after receiving aid, they were even punished. Many legislators today continue to blame our society's neediest when they can't repair their circumstances. For example, politicians openly denounce individuals who, through no fault of their own, are unable to pay for their health care when they are part of the working uninsured, or laid off from their jobs.

The basic Old English Poor Laws tenet that decides who is deserving of assistance, runs parallel to current-day social welfare policies. Stretching funding, in addition to political agendas, places less fortunate individuals on a "worthy of care" roulette wheel. Further stressors are placed on social service organizations, as administrators are left to decide what services will be cut, leaving needy persons to struggle.

The entire system is set up as a blame station when, because of fickle decision-making, society's problems continue unsolved. Blame is often handed off, and trickles down the social welfare food chain. It's a huge stressor as it cuts a wide destructive path, affecting workers and clients. Further, higher bars are set for both groups in order to meet tougher outcome goals with less funding. Gradually, the social services work culture begins to mirror the hopelessness of the people it serves; reflecting back to the Old English Poor Laws that state that change is inevitable because former efforts remain insufficient.

Following the American Revolution

When the states became one nation, social service need grew along with immigration, and the industrial revolution, that created a larger urban population. Beginning in the early 1800s, states took on responsibility for providing relief to the needy. Yet, private benevolent societies and self-help organizations began to form in response to the government's inability to sufficiently address social problems. Both private and public social service sectors emerged at that time, and have continued through today.

In the first part of the nineteenth century, John Van Ness Yates led New York to establish a "poor house plan" to build and maintain almshouses for the poor. New York City, for example, had become a settling place for immigrants, and cultures converged to create a new working poor. Volunteer "visitors" became part of the benevolent movement to provide assistance through direct relief and prayer. These visitors, who were mostly upper-class female volunteers striving to impugn Christianity and charity into the lives of those less fortunate, formed the "backbone" of the movement. Their work focused on moral persuasion and personal example.

In furthering the cause, the social welfare leader Dorothea Dix in 1841 brought to light the need to address the terrible sanitary conditions that existed for children, prisoners, the mentally ill, and the disabled. Volunteers continued to lead the social welfare mission during the Civil War through the Sanitation Commission and the Freedman's Bureau. The Sanitation Commission laid the foundation for the Red Cross and Public Health. The Freedman's Bureau, although short-lived, worked with newly emancipated slaves to ease their assimilation into society as freed people. The evangelical spirit permeated these organizations as well.

Throughout the 1850s and continuing through the 1860s Dorothea Dix's earlier reforms led to construction of public buildings. As a result, hundreds of reformatories, prisons, mental asylums, and orphanages were built throughout the eastern United States.

But the problems that created these institutions continued to go unresolved. State board movements were formed to solve them, and sought to bring organization to their state's institutions. Beginning in 1863, states began appointing boards to oversee and manage the operations of their institutional structures. They carried a variety of names such as State Board of Charities, Board of Public Charities, and Board of Corrections. Eventually, these boards began to prohibit proselytizing and discrimination based on one's political persuasion, religion, or nationality.

Rapid industrial growth in the latter half of the 1800s expanded community and individual social service need. Economic depressions, known then as panics, as well as new forms of racism, emerged following the end of Reconstruction. In addition, millions of Southern and Eastern Europeans fled their countries for a better life in America, but often found themselves in poverty as they sought work and experienced terrible living conditions and prejudice.

Complex Problems Lead to More Than One Right Way of Doing Business

Social unrest accompanied immigration influx and the antislavery movement. With the advent of, and following the Civil War, a volunteer work force was challenged to meet the need and support cultural and social assimilation. Basically, the country became a melting pot of races, religions, and cultures. But using only one approach to social work, or reform, didn't meet the needs of the population, although most people continued to assume that it could.

Consequently, two general social service advocacy movements emerged in the 1800s, and still exist today, each contributing greatly to the field. One group focused on case management with individuals and families, while the other focused on a larger picture of group work and community organization.

While the first of these reform movements centered on case management and developed the first professional social work practices, the second group grew into national organizations that advocate for national advocacy standards and policies. At times, one reform or another has been weighted to the detriment of the other. For example, a politically inclined administrator can make inroads with regard to state policies and standards, while neglecting evidence-based good case management at her organization. (Bullies will emerge when gaps in the service delivery system become blind spots for administrators.)

One Social Reform

Out of the chaos brought on by the economic depression and strikes of 1873, local social welfare advocates worked to address the problems of poverty, unrest, and destitution by expanding their local relief efforts. As a result of what they experienced as inefficient and poorly organized relief efforts, some social welfare reformers sought to regulate public relief distribution through something they called "scientific charity." Their strategy was to use the same blend of science and business efficiencies that had previously been used by state boards to avoid spreading "dependency and pauperism." Their basic principles included:

- Avoiding dispensation of direct relief. A founder of New York's charity organization, Josephine Shaw Lowell, was once asked by a donor how much money would go directly to the poor and she replied, "Not one cent!"

- The use of exchanges or registries as central recordkeeping systems that kept track of almoners, and prevented the indigent from receiving relief from more than one agency.

- A belief that poverty could be eradicated through the introduction of planned techniques and treatment plans. These interventions would be performed by "friendly visitors" imposing Christian charity and values. (Many visitors did authentic good works, and set the stage for what would become professional case-management.)

In 1877, the first American charity organization, Charity Organization Society (COS), using this scientific approach was founded in Buffalo, New York. But much of the approach was not successful with clients who needed help from within their own unique cultures and communities. And many of the "friendly visitors" were ignorant about the needs of their clients, while superimposing their own mores and values onto them.

Over time, societal problems began to be viewed by some "visitors" as more complex than their skills could handle. Many of these individuals, again mostly women, brought forward greater awareness that helping others required an education, training, and even salaries. But, it would be a while before the idea of professional social work caught on. It would be 1898 before "friendly visitor" volunteers would be replaced by paid caseworkers trained at the newly established New York School, later to become Columbia University School of Social Work.

Case Management and Friendly Visitors

During the course of its history in the United States, social service case management has been performed by differently skilled individuals, first by volunteers, then by paraprofessionals, and eventually by trained professionals. Volunteers and paraprofessionals continue to play a large role in social welfare. In the past, and up until today, the manner in which they play their parts can reveal much about how they effect change.

Another Social Welfare Reform

Other social service reformers introduced a social service model that became a type of urban mission. The Neighborhood Guild in New York City was established in 1886. Three years later, another, Hull House, was formed in Chicago by Jane Addams and Ellen Gates Starr. Settlements focused their attention on the environmental causes of poverty, and expanding work opportunities for the poor. By 1910, there were over four hundred settlements. Settlement work contributed to establishing the juvenile court system, pension programs for widows, anti–child labor laws, new research, the concept of social insurance, and public health reform. Eventually settlement advocacy led to the creation of national organizations such as the Urban League, National Consumers' League, Women's Trade Union League, and the National Association for the Advancement of Colored People (NAACP).

Parallel Reforms Working for the Same Cause

At the same time, the COS focused on casework as sub-specialties grew from their efforts. These included social work, medical care, and mental health care. Casework grew into formal social work training.

Dr. Abraham Flexner, an authority on professional education, stimulated further social service professional development when he gave a lecture in 1915 on the lack of technical skills and specialized knowledge in the field. The profession was growing as a result of World War I and the need to assist returning soldiers. By the 1920s, social work had become an established work profession in the United States.

Working in parallel, and with the same altruistic intentions, casework and community movements continued in the years that followed, and continue today. Dozens of social welfare programs formed the New Deal, generated from the Social Security Act of 1935. During and after World War II, further refinement of social service training and practices progressed. The Department of Health, Education, and Welfare was established in 1953.

It is interesting to note that primary beneficiaries between 1940 and 1960 were white middle-income workers. Gradually, voluntary and public sector organizations shifted their focus to low-income people within diverse populations.

In 1964, President Johnson's War on Poverty initiative took hold through the Economic Opportunity Act, which developed Upward Bound, Job Corps, Community Action, Head Start, Legal Services, Foster Grandparents, and the Office of Economic Opportunity. In 1965, Medicare and Medicaid, the Department of Housing and Urban Development, the Older Americans Act, and the Food Stamp Program were enacted.

The Elementary and Secondary School Education Act equalized education opportunities for children, and in 1966 the Model Cities Act emphasized the concept of community control by targeting certain urban areas with comprehensive services.

In the 1970s, President Nixon shifted the administration of anti-poverty programs to states and localities, and as a result, the State and Local Fiscal Assistance Act and the Comprehensive Employment and Training Act (CETA) were passed. During the Nixon administration, the Social Security Amendments of 1972, which centralized and standardized aid to disabled people and low-income elderly, and indexed benefits to inflation, were also passed.

In 1975, Title XX of the Social Security Act was passed and reinforced federal revenue sharing, which provided states with flexibility to plan social services and prompt fiscal accountability. During the Ford and Carter administrations, Title XX guided both public and nonprofit social services focusing more on welfare dependency that included child abuse and neglect, domestic violence, drug abuse, and community mental health.

The Carter administration, to address greater need to help children in poverty, created block grants that combined formerly categorical programs into wider programmatic areas, while establishing a ceiling on total state expenditures in return for increasing state control of spending patterns.

During this time, considerable changes and advancements occurred in the area of social work that included greater awareness about diversity and cultural disparity. This new awareness led to advanced course content, and efforts to recruit minorities into the social service profession. The growth of multidisciplinary and joint degree programs emerged as well. In addition, the field saw more private-practice development, and recognition of the BSW degree for entry level work in social work.

The Reagan years, in the 1980s, prompted social service advocates to rely more heavily on private-sector solutions for social service problems. At the same time, ballooning federal deficits prevented any new major social service initiatives. Consequently, by the end of the 1990s, there were 36 million Americans officially listed as "poor." As new social welfare challenges increased with cutbacks, as well as through substance abuse, HIV/AIDS, domestic violence, and homelessness, workers focused on building management skills and ramped up their advocacy.

By the time the Clinton administration came on board, focus was on inherited deficits and financial restraint. In 1996, AFDC was replaced through the welfare reform bill by block grants to states that included time limits and conditions on the receipt of cash assistance (referred to as Temporary Assistance to Needy Families, or TANF).

Political gridlock marked this social welfare era, while major social welfare issues went unresolved. Within the social services profession, administrators and workers were challenged by gaps in service provisions, and the advent of managed care. One bright light was the introduction of Americorps in 1994, which promoted greater involvement of young people in communities.

Then and Now

Throughout its history, social welfare has remained faithful to the New English Poor Laws (an outgrowth of the Old English Poor Laws), created centuries earlier. Workplace troubles such as bullying have often begun as a result of underlying assumptions about human beings, and their entitlements and rights. Once targeted toward clients, the New English Poor Laws have bled over to the workplace, through workplace bullying. These factors include:

1. See-sawing power between federal, state, local, and faith-based entities—Federal, state, and faith-based politics have dictated varying power-based social welfare agendas. Comparing Franklin Roosevelt's social welfare policies with Ronald Reagan's pretty much says it all, with religion continuing to figure in the picture, even during the twenty-first century.

2. Continuous change—Social service structures continue to bend to shifting policies and funding. They are required to reprioritize, sometimes on a weekly basis. Workers struggle to adapt, become exhausted, burn out, and risk behaving badly.

3. The thread of blame—Policies, programs, and individuals are continuously blamed for their weaknesses and missteps. Someone or something is usually a target on the merry-go-round, and in spite of the best efforts, remains blamed owing to rotating agendas. Celebrating successes runs a distant second to "What is wrong with you people?"

4. Financially trying to squeeze blood out of a turnip—Just as the Poor Law was instituted to keep the cost of "helping" down, the same principle holds true for current program- and worker-funding policies and cutbacks, based upon politics and budget priorities.

5. Deciding who is worthy of receiving help—"Are you worthy? If so you'd better prove it." This implied message could apply both to those being helped and helpers within the social service arena. In both cases, those making these decisions are often ill-equipped through their own ignorance, or through their lack of compassion.

In the twenty-first century, the work of social service continues, as social welfare policies rotate in importance. Stand in one place long enough, and a policy mandated ten years ago will come around again. It will be messaged as the "latest and greatest" policy, in tandem with the latest and greatest leader who replaced the former latest and greatest, but now forgotten, leader.

8

Who's Driving the Bus?
Bully Administrators in
Social Services

Drive—"to force to go, or push forward" (*Webster's New World College Dictionary*, 1999)

Introduction

Let me introduce this chapter by saying that there are very good social service administrators grappling with huge responsibility while leading their organizations like champs. This chapter, on the other hand, discusses social service administrators who have more or less lost touch with their clients and employees for many of the reasons described in Chapters 1 and 2. They hold onto their jobs through fear-based management strategies and behind-the-scenes machinations, both of which contribute to workplace bullying.

Social Service Administrators Weigh In

In writing this book I spoke with social service leaders who weighed in on administrators who have not recognized or addressed workplace bullying within their own organizations. Some of these leaders were genuinely dumbfounded as to why their peers could bully or allow bullying to occur. As one former COO of a large corporation, who is now a government social service administrator, stated, "I believe that people who enter this profession do so with the best of intentions, but bullying in social services is really odd. When I came to this field I was surprised by how ineffectively administrators used their power."

This administrator went on to say that she was unaccustomed to fear-based workplace cultures. Instead, she believes in cultures of learning. She also believes that in social services, administrators and managers are quick to blame, when what they need to do is ask questions (personal communication, March 3, 2011).

Another social service COO spoke about her own bullying experience when she worked at the White House. On her second day on the job, an older female staffer "called me out by saying I was not dressed appropriately." The older woman was establishing hierarchy, and even called this woman's supervisor to suggest that the younger woman, who, by the way, is a former beauty queen, needed to take classes on how to dress at work. The recipient of this bullying reflected that she was hurt and disappointed. She'd hoped to engage with a female mentor since the White House, especially at the time, was a more male-driven environment (personal communication, April 27, 2011).

Still another social service leader adds that workplace bullying starts with administrators who are required to push negative policies down the food chain, and while doing so, focus more on punishment than solutions. In her experience, she's observed bullying more from males than females. Her personal targeting occurred when she occupied a position alongside an explosive COO. He psychologically punished staff when they did not share his ideas. She stated, "I had to strategize how to do my work and still get around him." She further hypothesized that many male bully administrators prefer to work with women because men may be less likely to be psychologically manipulated (personal communication, April 18, 2011).

"Bullies are Incompetent and Obvious"—A Dubious Stereotype

Bully administrators are not altogether incompetent. And some very nice social service administrators lack competence. Administrators who adopt bullying as part of their management approach can be mean-spirited, ambitious, and driven to "win" at great cost to their employees, but they are not without competencies. Many bully administrators in social services are talented individuals with impressive backgrounds. They may combine business acumen with social service experience, but their larger flaws have more to do with a lack of empathy. For instance, they may have the ability to envision, think strategically about, and commit to a plan; but they lack skills in team-building, communication, changing organization orientation, and effectively managing staff. Instead, they resort to shortcuts, and manage through intimidation, fear, punishment, secrecy, blocking others from doing their best, micromanaging, and taking credit for other people's work.

One prominent trait shared among administrators who bully is the ability to be charming as well as politically astute. They can charm their board members, being superficially humble or overly deferential to the right politically placed people. Yet, with staff, their demeanors transform into mean-spirited and aggressive behaviors.

As mentioned previously, there's a good chance narcissistic social service administrator bullies view themselves as individuals who have the capacity to imagine larger visions for their organizations. And their visions play into how they rationalize their behaviors toward employees. For example, they may think cutting pensions will help save on organization expenses. And they are right, but the money they save will also fund their own yearly bonuses. It may not occur to them to consider that the money saved could fund cost-of-living increases for frontline staff.

Social Service Leadership—Management Theory X and Y

Leadership theories abound, but one seems to apply more to administrative bullies within social services. In his book *The Human Side of Enterprise* (1960), the American psychologist Douglas McGregor proposed his X-Y Management Theory. McGregor's theory suggests that there are two fundamental approaches to managing people. He felt that one management style, X, produced poorer results compared to the Y style, which reflected more enlightened management.

Bully administrators tend to adopt characteristics of X management style within vertically structured organizations that make the following assumptions:

- The average person dislikes work and will avoid it if he/she can.

- Therefore, most people must be forced with the threat of punishment to work toward organizational objectives.

- The average person prefers to be directed, to avoid responsibility, is relatively unambitious, and wants security above all else.

Whereas, the Y management style espouses:

- Effort in work is as natural as work and play.

- People will apply self-control and self-direction in the pursuit of organizational objectives, without external control or the threat of punishment.

- Commitment to objectives is a function of rewards associated with their achievement.

- People usually accept and often seek responsibility.

- The capacity to use a high degree of imagination, ingenuity, and creativity in solving organizational problems is widely, not narrowly, distributed in the population.

- In industry, the intellectual potential of the average person is only partly utilized.

The X-style managers and organizations are more autocratic within their work cultures and in management styles. Communication within the organization flows downward through external controls. The X manager acts as judge, and focus is on past performance. In reviewing workplace bully characteristics, it's easy to see why they can be identified as X managers.

X-Style Manager Traits

Bully administrators may claim one or more of these X-characteristic traits:

- Intolerant

- Short-tempered

- One-way communicator

- Vengeful and recriminatory

- Thinks giving orders is delegating

- Shouts

- Aloof and arrogant

- Detached and distant

- Does not thank or praise

- Results- and deadline-driven to the exclusion of everything else

- Is not a team-builder

- Elitist

- Seeks to blame

- Demands, never asks

- Holds on to responsibility, but shifts accountability to subordinates

- Withholds rewards, and suppresses pay and remunerations levels

- Does not participate

On the other hand, Y-style management does not hold to the belief that avoiding responsibility is an inherent human quality. It assumes that physical and mental effort involved in work is natural, and that individuals actively seek to engage in work. It also assumes that close supervision and the threat of punishment are not the only means to motivate employees. Y-style management espouses that, if given the opportunity, employees will be self-motivated and complete work goals. The ability to be creative and innovative is within the larger, not the smaller, population. In addition, individuals value recognition and self-esteem as work rewards, more than they do security.

Critics of the Y management style believe it is manipulative, and conflicts with how managers need to seek productivity rather than measures of employee well-being. They believe that workers, who are manipulated into working harder with the same pay, will not be satisfied until they also share in the economic benefits.

The Story of Madison and Ben

Once upon a time . . . Madison and Ben graduated from college and went to work in social services. Both individuals were very motivated to make a difference in their communities, and saw the value of their work. But while Madison and Ben shared the same reasons for getting into the field, they were different in other ways.

Madison came from a wealthy family and was brought up with the attitude that helping people less fortunate was a noble role in society. She wanted to do research to find out why people behaved in ways she thought deplorable, and felt that her contribution to social welfare could be more about her leadership skills than her actual work with clients. She soon found her niche when she landed a job at a burgeoning nonprofit organization. Through her strong desire to control and her urgent need to make more money she propelled herself into a management position.

Ben was supported by family to help others as well, and when a baseball injury sidelined his dreams of becoming a professional ballplayer, he found himself working with social service clients. He grew bored with frontline work after a year or two, and his natural charm and sales ability soon led him to management positions as well.

Madison felt that, owing to her innate cunning and visionary skills, she was destined to do great things, receive the recognition she deserved, and make a lot of money. With a knack for identifying and grooming potential wealthy board members, she became very good at developing donors. At the same time, she assembled talented individuals who knew how to write grants and supervise staff.

At times she ran into opposition when employees complained, but paid them no mind. When this occurred she simply ignored them until the problem went away, and iced out the individuals who brought the complaints to her attention. She didn't mind receiving the credit for the work of others, and, when she made terrible work mistakes, figured out ways to paint herself in the best possible light. She believed that her position exempted her from fault. Subordinates were always around to blame; usually behind their backs. In her mind she was above reproach, and focused on connecting with the community movers and shakers. Much like her early social-welfare predecessors in the eighteenth century, she superimposed her mores and values onto staff and clients, thinking she was the best judge of what they needed.

While Madison was attending to societal needs, and dressing to beat the band, Ben was growing in his popularity. He was handsome, charming, and had the ability to hire ambitious and aggressive staff, willing to pay attention to details. He genuinely liked people, and was effective at developing strategic plans. He quickly moved on at the beginning of projects. Details bored him, and he wasn't good at identifying them. Yet, he was able to deal with conflicts in a calm and relaxed manner. Ben also wanted to make money, and knew that his engaging style and authentic concern for clients and employees would help him attain his professional goals.

Which of these two administrators is more likely to become a bully administrator?

Madison is more easily identifiable as a bully administrator. Yet, Ben, by virtue of his hiring practices, could find himself surrounded by potential workplace bullies if he fails to pay attention to how his managers handle staff. As a "like-to-be-liked guy," he could value his staff admirers to the point where he overlooks legitimate work mistakes. In addition, because he has a tendency toward laziness, he could allow his organization to become stale (succumb to inertia), lose valuable new talent to bullying supervisors, and keeping favored employees who followed up on details in the wrong positions for too long. Longtime supervisors, working within organizations where inertia has taken hold, may feel threatened by newly hired and extremely qualified coworkers. Consequently, while Madison is the frontrunner as the administrative bully, Ben isn't far behind in potentially setting up a bullying workplace culture.

Dealing with the Boss Can Feel Like a Slow Boat to Crazy

Managers readily agree that working with human beings within complex social structures is less predictable and more difficult than operationalizing a learning management system, for example. Lawsuits against social services organizations happen because of human error, not often because of computer error.

Pulling together innovative groups of professionals with varying personalities in order to address client needs is complex work. Yet, great expectations rest with these workers and supervisors to turn the boat around in fairly short order, when it comes to addressing changes in new policies and programs. Social services organization administrators require a great deal from their frontline staff. It verges, at times, on magical projection.

One Psychologist's Cruise

A veteran psychologist experienced this unreasonable projection at her new agency. She was hired as the clinical director for a large, northeastern residential-treatment program that serves disturbed youth. This psychologist had already known her new boss was a charismatic CEO, but wasn't prepared to encounter his bullying when she was called to his office after six weeks on the job and dressed down for not turning the clinical program around.

During the boss's tirade he completely forgot to take our psychologist's expertise and experience into consideration when he questioned her ability to change an entire system of care into a shiny new program within six weeks. Yet, this same person found time at work to hang out with his favorite senior managers without paying attention to a strategic plan and implementation timelines.

After a few years at the agency, our psychologist requested vacation time after working two weeks in a row with no weekend break. Her boss said no.

"So much for rewarding fidelity and loyalty," she thought. As her workload grew overwhelming, she struggled to identify allies and backstabbers within the organization. She became acutely aware of staff morale, and eventually found the courage to tell her boss that staff were exhausted and feeling unsupported by upper management. While demonstrating courage, this was not what her boss wanted to hear.

As she looks back on her experience, our psychologist reflects that she made a mistake by staying at the organization too long, trying to make a difference. But, like many of her colleagues, she had a young family to support. She regrets letting her private practice go when she took the job. At the time, leaving her clinical director position would have meant giving up family benefits and jumpstarting the private practice.

Then, to her amazement, her boss left the organization, only to be replaced by another charismatic person, a very politically astute older woman without a lick of common sense when it came to thinking about the details behind her grand visions. Again, policies and procedures needed to be changed per the new administrator, and she found herself turning once again into a pretzel to accommodate a narcissistic leader.

Follow-Up

The recipient of the aforementioned treatment continues to weigh in on social service bully administrators. She believes that different social service organization leaders often mimic the behaviors and problems demonstrated in their client populations. For example, her agency's youth were receiving treatment for sexual aggression. Ironically, one of her bosses had the same issue.

Our psychologist has a point. Many professionals working within the drug and alcohol treatment field, for example, have had their own share of addiction problems. And child-welfare workers have often experienced personal childhood neglect or abuse. The same holds true for domestic violence survivors. Problems occur when social service administrators take little time to reflect on the possible connection between their earlier life experiences and how it may affect their current work. One wonders if this is a chicken-egg scenario. For example, are administrators with backgrounds similar to their clients drawn to the field for conscious or unconscious reasons—perhaps for some, a desire to make a positive change around past emotional pain? Or do they assume some of the same characteristics as the client population by virtue of the fact that they've been exposed over time to individuals with the same issues?

Our contributor also observes that stress plays a key role in how administrators behave within their work environments. Core behaviors easily emerge when conflicts and stress are present. Social service administrators would rightfully contend that there is plenty of stress in running their organizations. Juggling budgets, identifying funding streams, appeasing board members and legislators, as well as keeping human resources practices on track, all while providing adequate services, can be very stressful. When their coping skills flag, administrators can become bullies. And a correlation exists between how social service administrators treat staff and how staff pass bullying on to clients and coworkers, taking a cue from their bully administrators to bully down the workplace food-chain.

Our psychologist further shares the example of her first executive director, who expected his organizational vision to be immediately understood and implemented. Yet he was unable to tolerate questions concerning his visions for the agency. Confrontation enraged him. During those rare moments when a brave soul spoke up, he metaphorically killed the messenger by diminishing the person's professional judgment within the meeting.

Narcissistic administrators frequently see themselves as "crusaders" and "special" because they can envision "a grand picture." Consequently, at our psychologist's job, a breakdown in communication occurred among senior staff when the challenged boss became "wrapped around the axle." She believes her former boss's characteristics reflected megalomaniacal narcissism, reinforcing the thought that bosses who bully can be poor judges of their own work.

Greed, Status, and Power Drive the Bus—Why Bullies Enjoy Driving

Understandably, most administrators enjoy the benefits of power and high income that go along with their positions, seldom willingly giving up their jobs. When people do attain positions of power, they quickly learn that living in the penthouse beats what they've earlier experienced. Most new workers have little awareness about how much the boss can actually earn. When they do become aware, it can trigger their own ambitions, and not in a good way when it causes them to engage in untoward behaviors with coworkers.

Salaries and Bonuses

It can be difficult to wrap one's mind around the fact that people with an eye toward making money work in social services. The best way to make money in this line of work is to become an administrator because the benefits are often quite good. And when senior managers are making more than six figures a year, chances are there are additional pension and bonus packages attached. It makes sense that administrators who began working in social services at fairly low salaries would not willingly give up their six-figure incomes and additional benefits. Social service administrators will go to great lengths to protect their positions. When their salaries, status, and power are threatened, they can become very aggressive.

While nonprofit social services administrators make more, they are careful not to disclose their salaries. It could upset the apple cart, particularly when frontline social service workers struggle to make ends meet. According to a September 8, 2011, article in the *St. Petersburg Times*, a starting salary for social workers holding a bachelor's degree is about $29,900 per year, and a mid-career median salary is $46,800. In contrast, in Florida, for example, nonprofit child-welfare administrators are making six figures, some over $200,000 per year. Across the country, social services CEOs can earn more than $300,000 annually.

On the social welfare policy merry-go-round, states that more recently adopted privatization social service models called community-based care (CBC), pay local administrators more for their nonprofit jobs than was paid to statewide government workers. Government administrators were paid around $100,000 annually for the same jobs that now pay many of the privatization administrators between $140,000 and $190,000. In addition, these community-based-care administrators receive yearly bonuses. In the Brevard County, Florida, privatization system, $90,000 was set aside for bonuses in 2011 alone. In the Broward County, Florida, system the administrator was paid $182,000. In Miami-Dade/Monroe counties the administrator earned the same amount in salary and an additional $18,000 in bonus. Yet Florida's governor makes approximately $130,000 (Kestin, 2011).

According to the director of Florida's Children First, Inc., a nonprofit advocacy group for foster children, these administrators are essentially being paid for doing a government function, but paying themselves an exorbitant amount of money (Kestin, 2011).

Social Service Privatization

At the beginning of this century, some states instituted newly privatized community-based child-protection systems of care (CBCs) for children and families. These systems applied for, and were awarded, state-funded contracts to oversee child safety within their local areas. Bottom line, these community-based programs are essentially "pass through" funding agencies that contract with local service providers. Consequently, state-government-run oversight was transferred to local community oversight.

Over time, many of these community-based systems have grown larger than originally intended, employing more people and blurring their role by taking over services. In other words, they've been allowed to hold back money to run their own systems, while many nonprofit local service providers have lost income for direct service.

Mentioned earlier in this chapter, community-based administrators make a great deal more than government employees who in the past did the same jobs. Smaller CBC administrators have paid as much as $150,000 per year to CEOs supervising only thirty to forty people.

Behavioral health organizations have been brought into the loop as well, and are now contracting with states to privately manage health care and mental health services.

Privatizing social services is a newer way of managing state social services funds, but in Florida, for example, advocates have not openly discussed how much more administrators within privatized systems are being paid. The advocates for privatization point out that children and families are receiving better care, but what they won't talk about is the fact that in other states, county, not central, state governments have done a very good job of managing children's services at less cost and with the same results.

One lone Florida county (an exception in the state), received a community-based care contract to manage its child-safety system, and repeatedly ranks higher in its performance outcomes without paying huge salaries to its administrators. This is due to the fact that this county CBC has been folded into the county's existing functional departments that come with no salary disparities.

Nonprofit agencies are notoriously closed-mouthed about how much their administrators earn. In a tough economy, one large child-welfare organization's leaders persuaded their board to authorize 20 percent pay raises for six senior managers, while other staff eventually received only a 2 percent cost-of-living increase. Administrators at this agency were relentless in messaging how hard they had worked to obtain these "raises" for their employees.

Bonuses have been a part of social services senior-management compensation for a while. What would happen if frontline staff, with high school diplomas and barely scraping by above the poverty level, shared in any profit? In my experience, frontline paraprofessionals often struggle with difficult clients, completing the most tedious tasks, and answering to any number of people, while dealing with revolving policies and procedures.

Administrators would argue that bonuses provide incentives to management so they can continue to deal with daily job challenges. Yet, greater turnover occurs among lower-level staff. In the long run, sharing even small bonuses with them would likely save organizations advertising, hiring, and training expenses when they leave. It would go a long way in creating a more worker-friendly social structure.

Pension Plans

In recent years, social service government and nonprofit organizations have been eliminating pension plans for employees and substituting voluntary 403(b) plans that require staff contributions. What administrators are not disclosing is that they and their senior managers might be contributing to an additional pension plan called a 457(b), whereby they create their own organization contribution guidelines. The 457(b) plans apply to nonprofit or government workers and provide significant tax advantages because contributions and earnings on the retirement money are both tax-deferred.

While social service administrators receive additional benefits, lower-level employees are usually given the choice to contribute personal income only to a voluntary 403(b) plan. The problem lies in the fact that many frontline workers cannot afford to sign up.

What Social Service Donors May Not Know

When nonprofit social service administrators rise to speak at Rotary Clubs, they are probably not telling prospective donors that they have arrived at the luncheon in a car leased to them by their agency. And, when they talk about funding cutbacks and continued donor need, they probably don't mention the fact that they haven't cut their own total salaries. (When asked if they took a salary cut, they may respond, "Of course." But what they may conveniently omit is they will be getting a compensatory end-of-the-year bonus.)

Nonprofit administrators, especially within vertically structured organizations, seldom disclose their total annual income. Salary schedules are often negotiated with other staff as well, and sharing this information among other employees might reveal inequities in pay and bonus distribution. My former employer would strenuously deny my lingering belief that one of the reasons I was targeted was that I happened upon salary schedules while researching a grant. I was unaware I'd entered the "sacred circle" without being invited. My knowing this information was considered "dangerous," even though I'd had no intention to disclose it.

Differences Between Leaders and Administrators/Managers

Administrator

- To manage or direct the affairs of a government, institutions, etc.

- To give out or dispense, as punishment or justice.

Leader

- To show the way, direct the course of, by going before or along with, conduct or guide.

Dictionaries define administrator and leader differently, but they often get confused as the same. Definitions of "administrator" include words such as punishment and justice, while "leader," by contrast, denotes persuasion or guidance. Administrator bullying does not reflect leadership. Many leaders exist in lesser positions than their bosses, yet they have acquired certain characteristics that lift them above their peers, and empower them to do what is in the best interest of their organizations.

Most social service leaders agree that to empower and properly lead, trust must exist within the workplace. Good leaders are honest, visionary, transparent, flexible, and able to establish relationships. They are open to hearing honest feedback, and role-model effective team-building. They practice an "open-door" policy, and strive to understand and address staff concerns. In addition, they actively work to create healthy social structures within their organizations.

Social service leaders behave the same behind closed doors as they do in front of crowds. What people do when no one is looking reflects true character.

Leaders hold to a standard of professionalism that includes:

1. Making sure that employees are given proper jobs, and are well matched with their positions.

2. Advocating for fair pay and benefits on behalf of staff.

3. Making employees feel that their efforts are recognized.

4. Making sure employees work with nice people.

That's all there is to it.

Beware of Charisma and Buzz:
Social Structure Dysfunction

Dysfunctional—"Unable to perform normally; impaired." (*Webster's New World College Dictionary*, 1999)

The Perfect Social Services Organization Does Not Exist, and Yet . . .

There is no perfectly run social services organization—just as all the known saints are dead. That said, dysfunctional agencies lose their ethical bearings when they ignore problems that lead them down a slippery slope.

Consultants are frequently called in to provide direction about how to alter the course of dysfunctional organizations after board members suspect that things are amiss, and/or whistle-blowers have nailed themselves to a cross. These consulting experts often begin by evaluating the culture.

Culture Change Can Be Difficult in the Context of Dysfunction

Culture, as it relates to social service workplaces, is the history of shared learning in social behavior and meaning, which has become stable—and strongly resistant to change. According to author Richard P. Rumelt, organizational cultures or structures do not change quickly or easily (Rumelt, 2011). Cultural transformation means changing its members' work norms, assumptions, organizational memory, and work-related values. When workplace bullying and mobbing become part of the work culture, imbedding change can be compared to turning a ship around in a small harbor.

In his book *Organizational Culture and Leadership* (Schein, 2010), Edgar H. Schein defines culture as "a pattern of shared basic assumptions learned by a group, as it solved its problems of external adaptation and internal integration, which has worked well enough to be considered valid and, therefore, to be taught to new members, as the correct way to perceive, think, and feel in relation to those problems" (p. 18).

He contends that surface, as well as deeper, assumptions occur simultaneously in workplaces. In general, new employees are taught the more superficial cultural norms such as the social service mission and organizational structure. But that which is at the heart of the culture will be taught to and practiced with individuals with more permanent status, allowed into the inner circle where secrets are shared.

According to Schein, culture is always striving toward patterning and integration. Culture includes:

1. Basic underlying beliefs and values, and

2. Assumptions that are taken for granted, such as espoused beliefs and values, which include mission, goals, and rationalizations; and enduring practices and observed behaviors.

Social service workplace bullying exists within dysfunctional workplace cultures where:

- There is a failure to recognize or appreciate workers

- Best practice has not been implemented

- Policies and procedures are inconsistent and/or broken

- Staff lack competence in required skills

- Ambiguity is constant

- Leadership has failed to recognize and/or address workplace problems

Workplace cultures become habituated through ongoing, patterned management practices. As new evaluation measures emerge due to changing funding streams and policies, social services organizations are constantly challenged to embed new practice into old patterns.

Other factors contribute to dysfunctional workplace cultures that incubate bullying. They include:

- The nature of the work

- Crisis orientation

- Half-formed ideas and faulty messaging

- Narcissistic personalities

- Secrets; lack of transparency

- Inertia

- Failure to behavior ethically

The Nature of the Beast

By the very nature of their missions, many social services organizations are fueled by crisis and stress that lead to dysfunctional workplaces. Clients, often in need of urgent attention, can't wait for the ice to melt or summer to arrive to receive help. Several crisis-driven social service programs come to mind. For instance:

- Rape crisis centers—A female college student calls 911. Police bring her to the rape crisis center to be examined and counseled. The student is in shock, and her emotions are flat. She needs immediate assistance from the healthcare staff, crisis counselor, and law enforcement.

- Domestic violence programs—A battered spouse must leave her home immediately after her partner has crashed into their bedroom, pulled her from their bed, and used the butt of a gun to make his point. Their terrified children run to the neighbors, where police are called. Not only is the victim in need of medical care, but child protective services is called to identify where the children will stay that evening, and a child counselor is called in to calm the children.

- Juvenile justice—A fifteen-year-old is picked up for prostitution. He needs to turn tricks in order to purchase more painkillers. He arrives at juvenile hall in withdrawal, and needs immediate assessment by a case manager and nurse in order to address his needs.

- Elder services—An eighty-five-year-old man is discovered by his neighbor eating dog food. She turns to the local senior center for help, and they call the county's elder assistance program. An intake worker arrives at the man's home to investigate, but the man refuses to open his door. Police are called, and the gentleman is eventually coaxed by the worker to open the door.

- Child protective services—An anonymous call to the child abuse hotline reports that children are being neglected as a result of their parent's long absences. The two youngest appear to be cared for by their five-year-old brother, who has been seen rummaging through garbage cans in the neighborhood. A child abuse investigator is mandated in a short time to investigate, assess, and determine the safety of the children. In turn, the police will be called, and another placement worker will identify a temporary home for the children.

- Mental health services—A young man is found wandering the streets of an upscale residential neighborhood. He is having a conversation with invisible antagonists, telling them that he doesn't understand their mathematical formula. A Neighborhood Watch volunteer calls the police. It becomes clear to them that the youth is hallucinating. Is he using drugs, or does he have a mental health disorder? They take him to the mental health center for stabilization and assessment, and his family is called by an intake worker.

- Drug and alcohol rehabilitation centers—A twenty-year-old college student is brought to a detox center by his parents. He is drug-impaired, and reports taking several milligrams of oxycodone that day. He has disclosed his relapse to his parents, after having just spent thirty days in a ritzy private rehab center. His parents can't afford more treatment; they are at their wits' end, and have brought him to the nonprofit detox center for help. His intervention team will include an intake worker, aides, nurses, a nurse-practitioner, counselor, and an M.D.

Crisis Junkies Contribute to Workplace Bullying in Social Services

Workers who thrive on adrenaline are often found working in social services. Social services frontline workers who respond immediately to intervene on behalf of those in need bring to mind SWAT teams thrust into the breach. Many times, their work interfaces with law enforcement and legal systems, in addition to communication systems. Their effectiveness relies heavily on everything working together to get the job done.

Over time, crisis intervention programs, existing on adrenaline, can break down because individuals doing the crisis work either become addicted to the rush or desensitized to the work. When one or the other takes hold, breakdowns occur within the social structures, and bullying can emerge. Results can include burnout and compassion fatigue in workers, characterized by high irritability and turnover, or . . . lack of caring and competent victim advocacy. In fact, clients often bear the brunt of crisis-junkie behaviors.

Because crisis junkies are not normally happy with being micromanaged, it can be difficult to rein them in. And when an entire workplace culture (such as a child or elder abuse investigations department) is composed of individuals who have become crisis junkies, it takes a mountain of effort to bring them to examine their intentions and behaviors.

Other Structure Functions That Add to the Stress

This may seem like a stretch, but it appears that individuals who don't work in social services may believe agencies run on good-hearted donors and dedicated altruistic workers. It may be surprising to know that many behind-the-scenes employees contribute to running these organizations. Support functions for the aforementioned frontline workers are needed to keep social services going. For example,

- Information communication systems must tie client information and documentation together, and be securely stored.

- Quality Management must check to make sure that work meets federal, state, and accreditation compliance.

- Billing must be properly submitted and collected per each grant, program service contract, and any other form of reimbursement entity.

- Human resources must advertise, interview, hire, and train all the folks who service the organization, and handle their concerns.

- Other personnel must identify, write, and submit grant requests, and/or fundraise.

- Senior managers must become involved at the state and local policy-making levels, as their agency's board members determine the direction of their organization.

- Other support includes legal and administrative support, in addition to building-maintenance, leasing, and repair.

To make a long story short, there are many moving parts that keep the doors open, and when there are several parts to a system, mistakes, communication breakdown, high stress, and worker turnover can occur. All of the aforementioned factors contribute to creating dysfunctional cultures, simply because there are many people and intentions thrown into the mix. A clinical director might not think it's as important to get the budget written as it is to see someone in immediate need. Yet the budget person is waiting on him to submit very important line-item expenses in order to forecast next year's total budget. The frustrated budget analyst screams, "For Pete's sake, we need your information now!" and the clinical director screams back, "And how do you propose to lessen my work in order to make that happen?"

Disparity in Mission Goals and Intentions Contributes to Workplace Bullying

Social service personnel in support positions don't always share the same mission, that is, the one on the mission statement. In fact, people in finance may have no client exposure, and a very different take on what it means to help others. Many administrators may not have had frontline work experience and, in fact, come from business or legal backgrounds. Their expectations for workers may be unrealistic, and far from client-focused.

In addition, human resources workers may need to fill a position as soon as possible and, consequently, overlook the most-qualified candidate, choosing another who can start immediately. Given the complexities of the workplace, sororities and fraternities can crop up, as workers take sides and stubbornly become aggressive or passive-aggressive with one another. As a result, they may identify targets as "not one of them," and proceed to ice them out of the communication loop.

For example, a director of nursing is hired at a drug and alcohol detox center. She's not a psychotherapist, but she has good people skills, along with common sense. Her presence, however, disrupts the existing nursing staff because they've gotten used to reporting to a director who is not a nurse; they've been able to practice in a marginal way. Their new boss arrives on the scene to discover problems in care due to sloppy oversight. She takes her concerns to her staff. The stage is now set for a showdown. The mobbing begins as the old guard teams up against one lone new employee, who can't figure out what all the fuss is about. The chances of her staying and working to fix the system diminish when she discovers she is not the first nursing director to be targeted, or unsupported by administrators.

Half-Formed Ideas and Faulty Messaging Contribute to Workplace Bullying

Social services organizations are often given short turnaround times to meet guidelines set by newly awarded grants and contracts. Politics also figures prominently in what type of, and where, start-up programs emerge when agency board members and contract managers participate in the planning and implementation process. Consequently, in racing against the clock to meet their goals, nonprofits can end up providing something that looks very different from their original plan, owing to hasty decisions and flawed communication.

For example, a grant is awarded to an agency that requires rolling out their proposed program within a short period of time. The newly funded program must focus on creating infrastructure while hiring and training new staff to fill the new positions. A senior manager is designated as its director. She has had little to do with conceptualizing and writing the proposal, and, in fact, is not that crazy about the newly funded proposal. Yet she's been given the assignment to start it up, and to meet all the grant contract requirements. The proposal may have included hiring experienced counselors to translate the proposed program into action. The director has never been a counselor or had a background in counseling, and believes it's just fine to pull counselors from other failed systems of care within the agency.

The consequences of her decisions result in a poorly implemented program that reflects flawed communication and insufficient data. Under pressure from her COO, the director hires a new clinical counseling supervisor to clean up the mess. Contrary to her title, the new manager runs the program like a howitzer during the Second World War. In fact, she begins to bully staff. They leave, and new people are hired. The clinical director hires "bulldog" counselors who are teetering on bullying their clients as well. As a result, the added faulty decision-making made by that program director creates bullies, who emerge and thrive within this new program.

Half-formed ideas regarding service delivery are often the brainchild of social service board members who share their enthusiasms with one another. Here is an example: Two politically connected board members have just read the greatest and latest book on leadership, and decide they want to push this particular leadership strategy through at the next board meeting. They buy books for senior managers, and outline how the program should be laid out to benefit the entire organization. Benefits will outweigh the cost, they vigorously assert.

Given that one of these boosters is the incoming board president, the organization's CEO caves and begins to beat the drum among staff about the value of said training. The strategy passes, and the board votes to "steal from Peter to pay Paul" in the operating budget in order to buy books and training for employees, who barely have time to blow their nose before the next crisis. Employees scramble to read the book and implement the leadership methodology, which may or may not conflict with their own leadership philosophies. In their minds, the new orientation completely changes the way many have been managing for years, and they're not ready to transform old habits.

Bullies and targets surface when either resistance or compliance to the new strategy follows. An expensive trainer is paid to train staff. She leaves after two days, and those workers who felt the training to be beneficial try as hard to change leadership practice. But inertia rears its head, and push-back from other staff begins.

Within three months, follow-up from senior management becomes less frequent as other day-to-day challenges emerge, while the original advocates for change inevitably cycle off the board. Staff turnover continues, and within two years, those instructed in the new methodology have either left the organization or fallen back into their old habits. The CEO is on to the next appeasement exercise. In the meantime, the agency has spent thousands of dollars on an ineffective program because of its failure to maintain fidelity to its leadership methodology. And good staff have left the organization because they became targets and/or burned out attempting to implement the new practice.

Narcissistic Personalities Contribute to Workplace Dysfunction and Bullying

Recipe for Social Service Workplace Bullying

Take one Narcissistic administrator,

Add a full cup of Grandiosity,

Stir in a pound of Ambition,

Followed by a healthy dose of Entitlement,

Mix together: Lack of Empathy, Disregard for Others, along with some available Charisma,

and

Simmer for as long as it takes to create workplace bullying

It's worth repeating: Narcissistic administrators and supervisors play a major role in creating bullying at work. As mentioned in previous chapters, narcissistic individuals working in social services organizations, ironically, lack empathy. And empathy cannot be measured (Hemphill, 2011).

A certain amount of healthy narcissism can help administrators motivate and inspire workers. But when narcissism takes on pathologic features, it can derail an organization from its mission, and promote workplace bullying.

In addition to a lack of empathy, other pathologic narcissistic features include:

• Grandiosity, or "I am very special, and probably more special than you." And . . .

  • "I have the power to make things happen without you."

  • "My problems are not the same as yours."

  • "I can probably do everyone's work better than they can."

  • "It's not my job to worry about the details."

  • "I'm the visionary for this organization. No one does it better."

  • "I control the board."

• Ambition, or "How do I get from here to there in the shortest amount of time?" And . . .

  • "Who do I need to befriend to get where I want to go?"

  • "I don't mind working longer if it gets me where I want to be."

  • "I want to make sure I get there before they do."

  • "What I lack in empathy I make up for in will-power."

Entitlement also figures prominently in a narcissist's personality makeup. For example, many narcissistic administrators feel that they're owed in some way, because they believe they've done wonderful things for others. In their minds, they're entitled to persuade their boards to give them huge pay increases and bonuses because they're more deserving. Narcissists think they should get a "pass" when they're called upon by human resources to rein in their obnoxious behaviors.

Narcissists believe their concerns are more important than the concerns of others. In their minds, they've suffered more deeply. It's normal to spend time with an administrator who recounts his or her entire vacation, without asking how the other person is doing. They forget important workplace celebrations, arrive late to meetings, text during meetings, and feel free to change everyone's schedule in order to accommodate their own. They believe it's okay to make promises without fulfilling them, and don't share the truth if it works against them. They believe they're entitled to better treatment because of their status, and come and go at their own whim. When someone else shares an accomplishment, they'll talk about their own, and/or forget to congratulate or thank staff.

Narcissists feel free to assume dual roles because they think they can do a better job. For example, at one organization, a human resources vice president was also hired by his agency on a contract basis to provide counseling. This person, because of his belief that he could do a better job than the other counselors, felt that this was entirely appropriate. It was a subtle way of bullying the program's director, who was left in the position of supervising a superior, one who happened to be in charge of human resources. The contracted V.P. failed to turn in paperwork on time and took it upon himself to speak with the COO about clients, without consulting the director. When the director took her concerns to her supervisor, they were discounted.

Narcissists also frequently disregard the needs of others. They'll give themselves raises before other, more deserving, individuals. They'll pay attention only to those who share the same views, and they feel free to take credit for other people's work. They take power away from others when others are doing better work, and will easily ignore coworker achievements when said achievements threaten to overshadow their own.

All in all, narcissism within a social services organization creates the perfect recipe for dishing out workplace bullying.

Organization Secrets Contribute to Workplace Bullying

Senior management in social services organizations should not always disclose to staff everything that's going on. For example, if there is a possibility that a certain program may or may not get funded, senior staff will not communicate this to their employees until the decision is imminent and they've established a backup plan.

However, there are times when administrators communicate false hope to employees in order to squeeze the last drop of juice out of them. This happens before employees are being cut, or bullied, out of the system. Secrets are the opposite of transparency. Secrets send a message that there are only a few trusted people who hold the organization together. Secrecy trumps transparency within a bully culture. Secrets denote deception, while transparency denotes clarity. Transparency occurs when people feel free to ask for, and then receive, the truth, no guessing involved.

For instance, the CEO and COO have an opportunity to behave in a deceptive or transparent manner when a position opens up for a chief financial officer. They must decide whether to choose between an existing, easily manipulated employee without a graduate degree, or an external MBA job candidate. Offering the position to a less-educated employee will likely win loyalty; and, if they choose a highly qualified MBA from outside the organization, the external candidate might blow the whistle on agency secrets, putting them at risk.

Administrators are notorious for having already identified the person they want to fill a position, but they are usually required to interview others as well. If their intentions are not honorable, they'll go so far as to hedge their bets by picking an interview committee partial to their favorite, and by identifying one deciding competency skill obviously belonging to the person they've already chosen for the job.

One particular CEO is known for engaging his staff in discussions of issues already decided by agency board members. "Aw shucks," his humble self-effacing manner is deceptive. Younger staff may believe in his "inclusive" discussions, but others have gotten to know the flavor of his Kool Aid, so to speak. He feigns interest in what others have to say, and continues to follow the predetermined path.

A problem with transparency is that it opens people up to criticism and exposes their warts as well as their attributes. Administrators who are leaders, however, have a knack for being transparent and sticking their necks out to good effect. It takes a secure individual to place him/herself in such a vulnerable position.

Social Service Inertia Contributes to Workplace Bullying

Mentioned in the first chapter of this book, inertia occurs when a workplace culture is stuck replaying the same old themes, over and over again. The culture should be archived. It simply doesn't change, in spite of consumer complaints, employee turnover, and terrible lapses in service. Changes include streamlining the system by adopting new practices, technology, and employee guidelines.

When social services organizations have no community competition, inertia by proxy takes hold, and they enter the inertia vortex. Many communities have only one designated social services provider, which stays years past its effectiveness because it's the only game in town.

Bullying and mobbing surfaces where organizations are allowed to go unchecked with regard to practices. Old-guard staff often bypass appropriate human resources guidelines while the administration looks the other way, because years of loyalty have created long-term friendships and alliances. Again, it's extremely challenging to change these environments.

Consultants are paid to identify and suggest changes to antiquated systems of care. Their jobs are normally to guide board members and senior management in the right direction. Yet, if there is not enough commitment to change, agencies will very quickly return to their former comfort level and faulty behavior patterns.

Failure to Conform to Ethical Practices Contributes to Workplace Bullying

Ethics in social services are not the same as mandated law. Legal regulations often equal only minimally ethical standards of behavior. Ethical administrators aspire to promote the most ethical behavior, while others may not share the same aspiration, and in some cases only seek to capture minimal standards mandated by law.

Social services organizations require much from their workers. Standards of practice include ethically protecting the public, and exhibiting good character within the process. Professionals grapple daily with these issues. The work requires them to use all three types of human intelligence:

1. General intelligence—Knowledge and skills

2. Emotional intelligence—Practical social and emotional application of one's intelligence

3. Moral intelligence—The ability to determine right from wrong is the exercise of an informed conscience that practices justice and kindness, knowing the pain of their opposites

Individuals who engage in bullying and mobbing at work are not moral thinkers, and are behaving unethically when they choose to harm coworkers. Conversely, when individuals choose to behave ethically, they are demonstrating moral thinking.

On the job, narcissistic behavior affects ethical attitudes and behaviors. When narcissistic administrators focus more on their grand plans, they may not be paying attention to staff indiscretions. In addition, their sense of entitlement excuses them from any wrongdoing—or so they believe. In fact, they are not inclined to consider either the rights or needs of others, or the rules that apply.

Administrators with avoidant personalities also contribute to supporting questionable workplace ethics. These individuals may be in high levels of management, but lack the skills to handle confrontation. They will go a long way to avoid directly communicating with staff, and avoid difficult discussions. They often assign someone else to be their messengers. Consequently, they'll engage in or ignore questionable ethical practice, because in their minds, if it doesn't come to light, it doesn't need to be openly discussed.

Addiction-impaired administrators and supervisors also contribute to workplace bullying. Drug or alcohol impairment is an ethical (and sometimes legal) violation, yet impaired individuals will continue to work, very often until caught—sometimes more than once. By virtue of their impairment, they are less focused on ethical processes within their organizations. One chief financial officer was reportedly allowed to work at his organization for years because he had made empty promises to stop his alcohol use. In the meantime, he bullied a number of employees while engaging in questionable actions that put his agency at risk for losing important funding.

Bullying and mobbing in social services are boundary transgressions. When bullies scream at coworkers, or are otherwise consciously aware of their bad behavior toward others, they are being unethical, as well as exhibiting a lack of good character. To purposely demean and/or undermine another employee in the workplace is morally wrong, and, without permission, superimposes one's attitudes and mores onto another. It is an unconscionable action that reflects an unsafe, dysfunctional system of care.

Building a healthy workplace culture through its social structures requires an organization to have ethical leaders and staff, who thoughtfully pull all the right elements together. The benefits of an ethical workplace outweigh the challenges, and result in better care for clients. Keeping one's eye on the ball requires clear and consistent messaging, followed up by clear and consistent behavior. Implementing the magic of a well-functioning organization will be described in chapter 11 of this book.

"In the end, the afternoon knows what the morning never suspected."

—Swedish proverb

Points of Change
Part I—Targets

"I found my voice and there are no words for you." (Author unknown)

Down and Out, But Not For Long

Being targeted at work was a five-alarm wakeup call for me, especially when my career was more than halfway over. Bullying in the workplace seldom goes away on its own, and so I was compelled to address my problem. In years past, I'd had laser-like focus on the job and little time to notice how my coworkers were being treated. I suppose there had been plenty who'd been through what I was now experiencing, but it felt as though my experience was isolated and that I was the only person taking it on the chin for reasons I could not fathom.

After a considerable amount of time and effort, I resolved my bullying by leaving the organization. I left knowing little more about what I'd done to receive such lousy treatment than I had when it began. I had my suspicions, but no one at the top would validate them. Human resources at this organization did not acknowledge the problem of workplace bullying. And, while I ran into the V.P. on my first and last days on the job, she never acknowledged my presence at all.

As I mentioned, I had always received excellent job performance reviews; and so, frustrated, my low morale was intact when I left, even if my overall experience had left me with more compassion surrounding the issue of workplace bullying. And when I say that I resolved my problem, I mean I no longer exposed myself to bullies at work. By the time I'd had my farewell lunch with the COO, I was numb and exhausted. Nightmares followed my exit, and I continued to grieve the disappointment of my hopes. It felt lousy.

These feelings, however, were transitory. Since my departure, I've had more time to become reacquainted with friends and family, and to sit with my new awareness of my experience. A couple of times at the new job, I've used the information I discuss in this chapter. If I'd known then what I know now, I'm not sure that I would have had to leave my former agency. This chapter provides workers with the tools they need to deal with their own bullying.

Getting Started

Almost every resource on workplace bullying mentions that bullies are not above lying or plotting revenge on folks who challenge their bullying, and that when targets have prematurely challenged their perpetrators without doing their homework, they have usually ended up with the short end of the stick. Remember, there has yet to be a law against workplace bullying in the United States, and knowing this empowers bullies. However, if targets carefully record incidents, dates, and incriminating information, they can begin to build their case against the offensive behavior they've received at the hands of their oppressors.

Identifying the Problem

The first step in addressing a bullying problem is to identify it. It helps to know the signs of being targeted. Previous chapters have identified several, but a review of this checklist should help. If you have observed bullying/mobbing, or experienced it firsthand as a target, think of the list provided as a guidepost.

Specific Affected Areas
Work

- I have been given work goals with unattainable timelines.

- I have not been thanked for work contributions.

- I have been given less responsibility regarding jobs, whereas I was previously the point person or project leader.

- I have been marginalized out of future work projects.

- I have been taken out of the communication loop on projects where I was previously very involved.

- My work has been devalued and minimized by coworkers.

- While my skill sets are more extensive, I have been pigeonholed to do only one job task.

- My work outcomes have been manipulated by bullies so as to not portray me in a positive light.

- While I have the skill sets and competencies, I have been passed over for promotion more than once.

- I have had a cut in pay and/or received a demotion, even though my work performance evaluations have been excellent.

Relationships

- My boss does not voice or message his support.

- My boss does not back me up when there are clear workplace issues creating barriers to my work productivity.

- I have been stabbed in the back by "frenemies" on the job. (These are individuals who approach us in friendship, but use our shared information to capitalize on their own opportunities.)

- Coworkers, for fear of losing their jobs, are unwilling to stand up for me when they know I have been wronged.

- I have walked in on coworkers gossiping about me.

- I have had supervisors tell me that I'm expendable.

- I don't trust my boss.

- Former employees are not held in high regard by senior staff.

- Coworkers have attempted to silence me from speaking about my experience, because they don't want to be implicated.

- I feel psychologically alienated.

- My coworkers and supervisors have taken credit for my work, and as a result have been awarded raises and bonuses.

Emotions

- I have left work many nights questioning my skills and abilities.

- I have been adversely affected by my boss's screaming and shouting.

- I have been hurt by comments from coworkers or supervisors.

- I find myself crying more often.

- I have been more irritable and have had trouble controlling my temper.

- I find myself becoming anxious Sunday evenings in anticipation of the work week.

- I have been frozen by others' sudden abusive behaviors.

- I feel unrecognized and devalued by my boss.

- I have been shouted at by coworkers.

- I seldom laugh at work.

- I have been more anxious and worried.

- I feel sad and depressed.

- I am embarrassed and feel shame about my treatment at this organization.

- I feel hyper-anxious.

Management Structure

- Boundaries are blurred as administrators override informed recommendations made by more competent and skilled staff.

- Decisions made in general meetings are seldom the decisions implemented by senior staff.

- My administrators do not share their strategic plans with lower-level employees.

- There is no legacy plan for my organization.

- The organization's board members are not given full information when they are asked to make decisions.

- Lower-level staff do not receive bonuses based on job performance.

- Behavior toward workers by managers is arbitrary.

- Administrators share confidential information about employees with their peers.

- Human resources does not perform due diligence with regard to worker complaints about bullying.

- Transparency, with regard to communicating mission, is nonexistent.

- Senior managers tend to listen and act on gossip and innuendo from their confidants, rather than pursue the truth.

- Senior managers promote bullying and mobbing among staff in order to redirect blame away from themselves onto others.

- There is much staff turnover among managers and lower-level staff.

- Senior staff lack empathy with regard to their employees.

- Supervisors feel free to speak badly behind their supervisees' backs.

- Staff is motivated by fear.

Health and Well-Being

- I have been sick more days than usual, from colds and flu.

- I experience stress headaches or migraines.

- I have had to see the doctor to diagnose stomach problems.

- I have disturbed sleep and/or nightmares.

- I am fatigued most of the time.

- I have gained and/or lost excessive amounts of weight.

- I have experienced heart problems and/or hypertension.

- It's been difficult to exercise.

- I feel restless and irritable.

- I have had more skin eruptions and rashes than normal.

- I have experienced greater hair loss.

- I am more vigilant, tense, and jumpy.

- People comment that I look tired and unhappy.

- I have been prescribed antidepressants.

- I have been smoking and/or drinking more than normal.

My Thinking

- I hesitate to answer a question, fearing that I will be dressed down in front of my peers.

- My thoughts become frozen, and I cannot provide quick answers to simple questions.

- I have trouble making decisions.

- I often become confused when asked a direct question.

- I anticipate being surprised and shocked.

- I blame myself for others' behaviors toward me.

- I continuously try to solve the question of why I seem to be targeted.

- Sometimes my memory fails me, particularly in a meeting with my bosses.

- I constantly question whether I should assert myself or accept my supervisor's verbal attacks.

- I find myself driving beyond my destination or get lost because I am distracted.

Certainly, an employee does not have to experience all of the symptoms above in order to identify as a target. Also, consider where you rate your stress level. If your level of stress has increased substantially over the past weeks or months because of your abuse, it's a pretty good sign you're a target.

Making Assumptions

Once you've identified yourself as a bullied target, it's probably safe to make one or more of the following assumptions:

- Assume your bullies will not change, and that there is even a good chance of their behavior escalating if they're not stopped.

- Don't assume that your boss or other supervisors will support you.

- Don't assume that human resources is looking out for your best interests.

- Don't assume that human resources doesn't have a clue about other bullying reports and doesn't know the laws, or lack thereof, with regard to workplace bullying.

- Don't assume that your work colleagues have your back and will support you.

- Don't assume that you're not expendable.

- Don't assume that your organization has a workplace policy against bullying/mobbing.

- Don't assume that someone will magically recognize that bullying in social services is wrong and come to your aid.

- Don't assume that because of your sparkling personality and good nature, your bullies will see the error of their ways. Remember, bullies generally view "nice" as weak.

- Don't assume that bullies really are good people underneath their narcissistic exteriors. They're actually self-absorbed and would just as soon roll over someone without giving it a moment's thought. They're mostly incapable of feeling guilt for their behaviors and will rationalize them.

- Assume that even in social services, people don't always enter the profession with the best of intentions; sometimes they get involved because they like control and money.

- Assume that if you contact a board member with your concerns, that person will immediately take the information to your boss, and you could be in big trouble.

- Don't assume that if you file a lawsuit you will win and it won't cost you a dime.

- Assume that in the workplace, bullies don't cooperate, or play fair.

- Don't assume that anyone working in social services behaves more in accordance with higher morals and deeper character than individuals who work in other professions.

- Assume that any self-effacing comments you make are used against you.

- Assume that bullies will steal credit for what you contributed to the workplace, especially if you praise them for their contributions.

- Assume that any hesitancy or quietness on your part communicates vulnerability to a bully.

Keep a Record

Keeping a record of your bullying is not the same as keeping a journal. Records include data, while journal-keeping implies a cathartic exercise. Keeping a record of bullying behavior you experience, along with the date, time, individuals present, type of encounter (whether it was a set or impromptu meeting), is essential. Along with this information, keep records of visits to your physician that include dates of visits that coincide with any run-ins with the bully. Is the doctor's visit tied somehow to the bullying?

For example, at a meeting you are dressed down by your bully, and that afternoon you need to visit your doctor because of a severe headache, or stomach issue. There may be a link between the encounter and an emerging physical condition.

As you record your information, identify your bullies. In my case they were mostly senior-level females. You will also notice behavior patterns that can emerge when you present some form of threat to perpetrators. In my organization, whenever I was getting ready to share a success, or an idea to promote innovative practice, my bullies became verbally abusive.

I recognized another pattern that emerged, when I was recognized for my accomplishments outside of the organization. My national magazine interviews went unrecognized, and when I was scheduled to speak at a national conference attended by coworkers, only one of my colleagues was present for my lecture. Shortly thereafter, the same person became part of my mobbing consortium.

When their behavior is called into question, bullies will first appear confused and then request specifics, so they can refute or rework the information in some way in order to rationalize or deny their behavior. Make sure the specifics have been written down. If one chooses to file a complaint with human resources about bullying at work, there needs to be a clean, well-documented record. Writing down one's responses that relate to post-traumatic stress symptoms can be helpful as well, but make sure they relate back to a specific incident. For example, a typical PTSD symptom is avoidance. So, if one notes that she or he attempted to avoid contact with a bully following an incident, an emerging symptom of PTSD is demonstrated. Attempting to redirect or avoid conflict after one has been screamed at during a meeting is another example. Remember, PTSD is simply a cluster of symptoms, and by recording your experiences and subsequent physical and psychological responses you can identify patterns that indicate emerging post-traumatic stress disorder, depression, and/or other types of intense anxiety.

Record your emotional responses as they relate to fear, terror, anxiety, sadness, and emotional pain in response to a bullying incident. Do not elaborate on these responses with judging statements, because they are generally viewed as subjective, and you could come off sounding weird and paranoid. A normal survival response to a bullying experience is "freezing," or reacting like a "deer in the headlights." Accompanying this arousal state is usually a sense of surprise, confusion, and/or bewilderment. Documentation about a verbal assault could be, "When Sam stated I wasn't qualified to do the project, I was stunned. My qualifications exceed what is needed for the project. I literally didn't know how to respond at that moment, and I froze, unable to make a rebuttal or assert myself." (Don't forget to record the date, time, and circumstance, along with the names of those present.)

Do *not* go through a mediation process with your organization. As with domestic violence, mediation is not a good avenue to follow to resolve your bullying. It places the target in a position of compromise when he or she has already been compromised. According to Loraleigh Keashly (Namie & Namie, 2011), mediation does not provide restitution for past acts against the target. In addition, a power imbalance has already been established with regard to the target and the bully because the target is the victim and the bully is not. Mediation is intended to mediate between equal parties. Bullying is a form of violence, and violence should never be mediated.

Preparation

There are steps to prepare yourself to address the bullying problem, even before taking action. Identifying yourself as a target is the first step in addressing your bullying. The following suggestions promote feeling psychologically prepared and safe.

1. Identify Your Support System and Examine Your Options

"Which way should I go?" was my mantra for a very long time. Given that my boss and his senior management team were not going to promote me or begin to consider me as an equal, I was kind of lost as to who could be part of my support system as I struggled through this experience. Luckily, I had made friends with other frustrated people who were still with, or had left the organization because of their own issues with upper management. (We did not tend to complain. We happened to see the same things at the same meetings and do some reality-checking with each other.) Even the organization's attorney weighed in (behind closed doors, of course) about his own treatment, but understandably could not come right out and openly support me, as that would have put him in a very awkward position should I decide to file a complaint with the EEOC (the U.S. Equal Employment Opportunity Commission).

Another workplace colleague and I became friends because we'd formed a book club together. As the organization's director of quality management, she was also in a compromised position knowing that management fell short, with standards for job performance and pay being arbitrary at best. With her husband out of work, and as the sole provider for her family, she walked on eggshells to please the powers that be, while they continued to pile on the work.

There were others as well, but all in all, I recognized that any substantive support would have to come from outside my job. My husband was very understanding, and extremely empathetic and supportive. My darling sister was always available as a sounding board and to share her wisdom. My young grandchildren provided unconditional love and laughter. My job coach was an authentic reality-check, and my minister was a compassionate spiritual guide. And my dear neighbor provided immediate debriefing support when I came home and needed to unload. These folks cared about and supported me, without risk of exposing themselves to harsh treatment from my employer.

2. Recapture Personal Control

The feeling of helplessness can be overwhelming for targets, so the sooner one gains control over something, the easier life can be; even if it means that you place new pictures on your office walls, or restructure your daily work routine to include lunchtime exercise. One of the ways to feel more in control of your situation is to acknowledge you have a choice to make when it comes to leaving your job. This was a daily consideration for me.

3. Take Some Time Off and Get Some Rest

For many years I've presented workshops on Workplace Compassion Fatigue and Burnout in Social Services. As one can imagine, there is always a need to address this topic in social services. In my workshops, I always discuss the need for rest before making important decisions, particularly when they relate to careers.

Being targeted is synonymous with taking a psychological beating, and it takes a tremendous emotional toll. Mentally preparing for the next surprise assault can preoccupy our minds when they should be at rest. The additional burden of trying to figure out something that just doesn't make sense takes a lot of mental energy. If you've built up leave-time over the years, and many targets have, it does you no good not to take it, in spite of your fears.

Many targets hesitate to take earned leave, or even leave without pay, because they're concerned about any surprises that will await them upon their return. If you've already been targeted, you need to take some time away to gain deeper perspective and take care of yourself. There is no rule that we should not take care of ourselves when we're abused, yet many targets punish themselves further, out of shame and guilt.

Rest and play are essential when we live balanced lives. Targets often forget to play as they go through their workplace bullying experiences. As a matter of fact, they frequently work harder, trying to prove their worth. Targets too often identify themselves through their work. Many social service individuals are fairly self-sacrificing (or they wouldn't have chosen their careers), and play can be challenging to people who've dedicated their lives to helping others.

Rest and play allow us to pause and take stock of our reality, as well as illuminate our blessings. We are able, through rest, to reflect more on our priorities, our spirituality, and our good luck. We can gain a healthier perspective with regard to the feelings of guilt and shame brought on by our bullying as well.

4. Assess Your Personality Type in Terms of Your Employer's Workplace Culture and Social Structures

I also had to examine my personality makeup, and how it fit with my workplace culture and social structures. Obviously there were some problems because my personality, as sparkling as I thought it to be, was not adapting very well to its environment. My emotional transparency simply didn't work with the close-mouthed, tight-lipped, and secret fraternity handshake shared among senior managers. So I had to continuously ask myself how I could reprocess my brain in order to fit in. This was tricky because time and again, I was forced to confront my rather magical hope that somehow I would be valued for my quirkiness. My job coach was constantly reminding me that any thoughts I had about changing the workplace culture were unrealistic. So think about how your personality matches your work environment, and whether or not you can accommodate it.

5. Identify Your Need for Professional Consultation

For more perspective and input about your options, think about working with a job coach or counselor to help sort through your own stuff and what is authentically occurring on the job. Never underestimate the power of one's erroneous thinking. It is very true that our brains are extremely powerful when it comes to our worldview and daily perceptions. We may think we're being targeted when, in fact, we are actually dealing with our own sense of inadequacy.

It helps to go over the signs of workplace bullying and your current psychological status with an impartial party. Normally, that would be a licensed mental health therapist. Be sure you choose someone versed in trauma-informed interventions, in additional to workplace bullying. If the person doesn't know that workplace bullying is serious, then you're not going to be helped. In addition, work with someone who knows how to reprocess your traumatic bullying memories through a technique called E.M.D.R., or Eye Movement Desensitization Reprocessing. And, should you be considering taking legal action, you need to ask your therapist at the outset if he or she has provided evaluations or appeared in court. Many psychotherapists are unwilling to work with the courts, simply because it can be a very harsh experience. Yet, there are others who have made workplace bullying evaluation and intervention a specialty area because they believe in the mission.

If you stay on the job, your therapist or job coach will help you strategize navigating through your experience; or should you decide otherwise, help you work through your grief, help you reprocess your experience, and support you in moving beyond your workplace bullying.

6. Learn More About Your Legal Options

Legal recourse isn't clear-cut, but it is still an option. Existing federal laws focus on the harassment/discrimination of those in protected classes such as race, religion, national origin, age, or disability. Since 2003, eighteen states have proposed a "healthy workplace bill" that holds an employer accountable for an abusive environment, but none has become law (Petrecca, 2010). Claiming discrimination requires EEOC permission (through a right-to-sue letter) before hiring a private attorney, because you must be a member of a "protected status group" to claim damages (Namie & Namie, 2009). In addition, while unions may forestall your employer's retaliation—and there will be retaliation—working in "at-will" states gives employers all the power to fire employees or cut jobs with little recourse for the employees.

Pursuing a legal case against your employer will cost you time, money, and more time. If you're considering taking legal action, remember that most attorneys have a difficult time grasping workplace bullying and pursuing cases because there are no existing state laws against it. One potential avenue is to claim "intentional infliction of emotional distress," but the standards to win such claims are almost unattainable. At this point, proponents of workplace bills emphasize physical and psychological harm done to the victims.

Most employment lawyers work on behalf of employers, so you will probably need to do some research through your local branch of the National Employment Lawyers Association to find someone who can knowledgably represent you. As far as cost, lawyers get paid three different ways: (1) hourly, in which case you pay as you go; (2) on contingency, in which a percentage of the winnings goes to the attorney if there is a victory; or (3) by retainer, wherein a deposit is paid in advance, and, should the case progress, additional money is paid.

Authors Namie and Namie (2009) remind targets that pursuing legal action places most of the burden for winning their cases on the targets. It can be a long uphill battle, leaving targets feeling even more abused and invisible. So carefully weigh the pros and cons.

Should I Stay or Should I Go?

This question has an awful lot to do with one's temperament, the job market, and the desire to keep your paycheck, status, and position, as well as your right mind. Sometimes, targets aren't given a choice, because eventually bullies will find a way to cut their jobs, and not pay unemployment compensation. They just make things more and more uncomfortable for their targets.

Basically, your choices are:

1. Staying at your job under the current circumstances

2. Taking action by addressing the problem

3. Leaving your job

Staying at Your Job Under the Current Circumstances

Think about what you would need to change within yourself if you were to stay at your present job and work with your bullies. Targets have managed to pull it off when they've had the ability to develop thicker skins, zone out when they're exposed to abuse, and address their bully's narcissistic needs. Some targets have been able to navigate into parallel positions at the same workplace in order to move further away from their bullies. Some examples:

> *Jack*—Jack was told he needed to develop a thicker skin and not worry about the "supposed" slights from his coworkers. So he chose to ignore them and appear unbothered by their teasing and put-downs. Every night, he stopped at the gym to relieve his frustrations through exercise and weight training.

> *Barry*—Barry created a wall of quiet around himself at work, following several run-ins with narcissistic bosses. He hated his job but needed it for the benefits it provided, and he felt he was too old to find another job that paid as well. Barry learned to avoid confrontation and, usually following one of his boss's tirades, closed his office door, put on his earphones, and listened to music, while he completed the newest urgently needed report. He counted the days and hours until his retirement, telling himself he was tolerating his abuse for the sake of his retirement security.

> *Jamie*—Jamie knew that her boss was an angry person, and extremely competitive with other female employees. She rightfully assumed that her boss would never give her work that would highlight her abilities. But Jamie figured out that if she could spotlight and flatter her boss, the boss might not be intimidated. Jamie played to her boss's needs and circumvented her boss's temper tantrums by being very apologetic.

> *Gail*—Gail was in a no-win situation because she had grown beyond her present job, but knew that her boss would not give her any more responsibility. He was jealous of her skill sets, and knew she was a serious professional threat. Gail assumed he would not allow the loss of his power and status

because of competition. And she was correct in her assumption. He began to diminish Gail's accomplishments to his peers by dropping subtle messages into seemingly casual conversations. Gail eventually got wind of his smear campaign and decided she would need to make herself indispensable to the organization, so that she could keep her job and transition away from her boss. She began to work on operationalizing several innovative projects that would provide value and income to her social services organization. In addition, she sought further training in accreditation supervision, in order to address organizational need. Eventually, with her new skill sets and programs she was made director of a new department.

Taking Action by Addressing the Problem

There are different ways to approach your situation, and it helps to utilize as many approaches as possible as you continue to record your actions along the way. Here are some recommendations:

1. Identify helpful influencers and ask them to advocate on your behalf. In my previous job, the influencers at the organization happened to be my bullies, but if there are people within your organization who can be your voice and take your problem to an even higher influencer, your bullying could be resolved sooner rather than later. My one attempt to get support from an influencer within my organization occurred before I knew he didn't want me around. I had genuinely believed he would help me resolve my problem because he branded himself "the humble guy," and many people believed his advertising. Betrayal is too light a word for what I felt upon discovering that not only was he not on my side, he was on "theirs."

You may know someone in a position to report your circumstances to the right people well enough that they will help. If you happen to know someone well who also is a great chum of your employer's board president, ask if he or she would consider communicating your experience to his or her friend. You might also work through a former coworker who is thought of highly by upper-level management, who will vouch for your integrity. She or he may gladly advocate on your behalf or gracefully decline, but it's worth a shot to ask.

Make sure that you know what you want to happen when you ask someone to advocate for you. Do you want a new policy written about workplace bullying, or do you want people to be called out on their behavior and apologize? How much time will you allow for an individual or the organization to take action on your behalf? Are you willing to take another job in order to remove yourself from the situation? Are you afraid of supervisor retaliation if your problems are taken to a higher level? Think about your answers in realistic terms, and don't waiver from them once you decide what to do.

With regard to an apology, think about how your bullies will consider their personnel files if they admit to wrongdoing and apologize. Will their admission follow them to other jobs? What if you want to sue them because you've developed a serious medical condition due to their bullying? You will be asked these questions and asked to carefully consider your answers. Remember to provide proof through records that substantiate your allegations. And inquire about when you might hear back from your advocate following his or meeting with those in power.

Be realistic and assume there will be push-back from your bullies when you obtain advocacy from a supporter. It may not show itself immediately, but narcissists generally have very long memories. On those rare occasions where bullies are relieved of their duties, or decide to share their love at another organization, you will be grateful for your advocate's support.

2. At the first sign people are gunning for you, call them out. You don't have to hit them over the head with a hammer. Just let them know you will not tolerate the behavior.

> *Kim and Shirley*—The first day on the job, Kim was informed by Shirley that Kim would not be using an office to see her counseling clients. Shirley stated that only she, Shirley, could use the one office, because she had been with the agency longer. Bewildered, Kim looked around and asked incredulously, "Where do you want to put me?" Without pausing, Shirley responded, "In the hallway cubby." Wow, thought Kim, this is really weird. How can I see clients in the hallway? And, yes, this is how Kim began her first day.
>
> On day two, Kim was instructed by Shirley on how to properly wind her computer connector lines together, so as not to damage them. Kim wondered when she was going to learn about her new clients, and when she asked, Shirley stated, "We're in the process of figuring out the system. But you shouldn't worry about those things."
>
> On day three, Kim was informed that she would not be allowed to hang or display any personal items because, Shirley explained, it would put marks on the

walls, and that wouldn't suit their landlord. (A few days later, Shirley caved and stated that if Kim wanted to hang any pictures, she needed to take pictures of them first for Shirley's approval. "I don't like those chopped up modern pictures," Shirley explained.)

On day four, Kim was informed that she would be taking only noninsured clients and that Shirley would see those with insurance.

On the fifth day, Kim went to their supervisor and inquired about her directives from Shirley. The supervisor clearly had an affinity for Shirley and stated that, while Shirley could be somewhat controlling, she was really a very good mental health therapist. Not having her questions answered, Kim requested that she, Shirley, and their supervisor meet to iron out the program practices. Three meetings were held, and two were attended only by Kim.

After two weeks, Kim requested comfortable chairs for the clients, and Shirley said there was no budget for that, and, oh, by the way, "Kim, I feel you think you're entitled." Without blinking an eye, Kim responded, "I think you feel entitled too, Shirley." Shirley's mouth opened and closed, and she huffed her way through the exit door. For the next few weeks, Shirley did not speak to Kim. Shirley's silence ended when Kim greeted her several times before Shirley responded.

At the next one-on-one meeting with her supervisor, Kim laid out the definition of workplace bullying to her supervisor, citing sources, as well as giving specific examples and dates of her encounters with Shirley. Next, Kim approached the human resources director and mentioned that, if the director would like, she would be happy to provide training on workplace bullying. Then, Kim informed coworkers when they inquired about her new job that Shirley's bullying held a workable solution.

And that it did. Within five months, Shirley left her alone, and Kim went on with her work, using the office to see clients, and decorating it with warm accessories. She also became a resource for the organization's newly written policy on workplace bullying.

3. Speak up to the bully in front of others. It can be very effective to speak up to bullies when they're doing their "thing" in a group setting. But there are some caveats in going this route. First, you want to make sure that you don't challenge a bully in front of his or her peer group and/or support system, especially if you are not at the same authority level. You will be creamed.

Second, make sure that you don't come off sounding like a bully yourself. You could end up with pie on your face, when the bully turns the tables on you. It could go something like this:

Target: "Jack, are you aware that your behavior could be defined as bullying right now?"

Bully: "Gee Herb, you specifically asked me to be direct with you. I'm confused about what you want from me? Do you want me to couch my comments or do what you asked?"

All that said, it can be effective to call your bully out in a meeting attended by supportive colleagues and/or employees at different-level positions within the organization.

This example illustrates a target and bully encounter:

> The target is the new kid on the block and intimidates the heck out of a colleague in a parallel position. As time goes by, the target's efforts at innovating their shared program threatens her bully, who begins to stonewall the target's efforts to make positive changes. As the target struggles to work with her staff, which had until recently reported to the bully, the bully ups the stakes by methodically antagonizing the target through his lack of response to her attempts at team-building. Finally, it all comes to a head at a staff meeting, where the target and bully sit across the table from one another. The bully has been accustomed to running the meetings, so he takes the lead with the meeting agenda and announces that anyone wanting to make programmatic changes will now have to go through his newly organized committee for approval.

> The target begins to take action. She calmly asks her bully why she was not asked to be part of the committee, since they share parallel program leadership functions. The bully answers that he didn't think the target had time to work on a committee. The target responds that she has plenty of time, and that she will serve on the committee, and plan to co-chair it with the bully. In addition, she requests, in front of the group, that any other decisions made should be brought to her attention as well. To top it off, the target might add, "I know we all want to avoid creating a bullying work culture, so it's great we can cooperate on this. Thanks so much." At the end of the meeting, the target will record her discussion by using factual statements. She will keep her

record in a locked drawer. In addition, the target may expect that this will not be the last of her bully's attempts to derail her, and she will share the interaction with her supervisor and/or trusted upper-level manager if it happens again.

4. Have a heart-to-heart with your bully. (Did I really say that?) If you choose to take a complaint to human resources, you will be asked if you've ever spoken with the alleged bully about the problem. If you haven't, you will probably be asked why, and you should have a pretty good answer, one that may have something to do with the word "retaliation."

Needless to say, remember to take a notebook with you if you do set up a meeting with your perpetrator. And it helps to get straight to the point by using "I" statements and specific examples, along with dates of your abusive encounters. You then ask your bully to cease the inappropriate behavior.

Of course, bullies have any number of responses when they're "called out" for their actions. Their responses can range from anger or confusion to recognition and apology. Because bullies don't see themselves (1) as bullies and (2) as flawed, their first response could be anger. Another likely response could be bewilderment: "What are you saying? I have no idea what you're talking about."

Yet another often used response is the counterattack. Bullies could likely counter your comments by saying something derogatory about you:

• You're too soft.

• You need a thicker skin.

• You're too sensitive.

• You don't understand the nature of the business.

• You're in for a lot of problems if you can't cope.

Be careful not to be put on the defensive. If your bully begins to hammer away at your character because you dared to call him or her out, record what the person says and take your information to human resources.

Should your bullies acknowledge and apologize, don't be surprised if they try another tactic to get to you. You could end up sounding like a whiner if they continue their behavior and you complain again. A calculated bully response to human resources could be, "Susie and I did have a conversation, and I did apologize. I'm sorry she's still holding a grudge."

There is a chance, however slight, that in having a heart-to-heart conversation the bullying can be resolved; especially if you talk about the workplace bullying, and through your research it looks like you've been targeted by the person who is sitting across from you. Talk about what's been learned and let the person know that this is a serious topic. You may even want to add that you appreciate him or her taking the time to speak with you about this important issue. Remember always to share specific examples and dates of your encounters.

5. Take your concerns directly to a higher-level authority. Upper-level management may not know that bullying is occurring within their organization. They may have been given false information or no information at all when a target has attempted to resolve the problem through the proper channels. If you haven't made any headway going the respectful route, try going to a higher level of authority for help. You should make no apology for following this path. Remember that bullying is a form of violence, and undeserved.

Again, make sure you have your ducks in a row when you meet with upper-level management. Vice presidents, COOs, and CEOs don't have much time for idle conversation. So get to the point. Share the research on workplace bullying as well as your specific experiences. Don't make excuses for, or judgments about, your tormentors. Share the facts, state how the experience has affected you, and request that the situation be addressed. Refuse a mediation meeting, letting the boss know that research recommends strongly against mediation meetings in this context, and give the reasons why. You will be asked what steps you want taken; have your answers ready. Make sure you bring a notebook, and if you feel safe, print a copy of the incidents for your listener.

If senior managers participate in the bullying, don't expect the CEO to be very supportive, especially if he or she has handpicked the staff and counts on their loyalty. You could be viewed as expendable, whereas they are not. It is likely, however, that the CEO or COO will pay lip service to you and your problem, and, as in Lt. Paula Coughlin's experience, promise immediate resolution.

Because my bullies were senior staff, my attempts to resolve my situation by speaking with the CEO fell on deaf ears. I was rerouted back to my main perpetrator, who then turned the tables on me. It felt like being caught in a vortex. Only when

I'd left the organization, and following considerable spiritual and professional consultation, did I speak to the board president. He was very respectful, listened, and said he would get back to me as soon as possible—and then never did.

But that doesn't preclude you from going to your board president before you feel compelled to leave. It takes great courage to seek out help from the top because the ramifications back at the workplace can be terrible; however, I do know someone who took that path with success. My colleague was able to convince the board president that too many shenanigans had been engaged in by the CEO, and the appropriate changes were made.

6. Begin a workplace bullying education campaign. Naturally, human resource departments steer away from discussions that may promote complaints from employees, but it could be worth your while to approach someone who has the authority to give the go-ahead to begin an education campaign at your organization. You can persuade the "permission granter" that it is in the best interest of the organization to write a workplace bullying policy that includes zero tolerance for the behavior.

You can add that workplace bullying is being further researched, and that the issue's status is similar to that of domestic violence before there was awareness about that problem. When the feds are looking to fund new programs or initiatives, part of a grant proposal includes the organization's mission, philosophy statements, and any other information that demonstrates an unbiased work environment. Point out that having a workplace bullying policy and education training in place can put the agency in a favorable light.

In addition, no senior manager wants to appear insensitive to this issue. A written policy, authorized by the board of directors, will spotlight the boss's sensitivity to his staff.

It can be argued that an anti-bullying policy will support staff retention, something every social service agency is concerned about. Having workers trained on the topic of workplace bullying and procedures for dealing with it are effective ways for workers to gain some feeling of control and means to address their concerns. Workplace bullying education can include brochures, focus groups, classroom or online training, certification training, and any other method or informational material that furthers awareness on the topic.

Remember, measured action is best. As you pursue various actions along this journey, keep your anger in check. Missteps can mean the difference between staying on the job and not having a say about your leave-taking. Unchecked anger is not a target's friend, although it is an authentic emotional response to the situation, as well as a great motivator. Work at keeping it under control so that there is no record of you behaving inappropriately during any time during your process of addressing the problem and/or leaving the organization.

For my part, I had done a pretty good job of keeping my anger under control, until after I had tendered my resignation. Still, I was pretty well fed up with one bully's personal and professional attacks. Having learned of another behind-the-scenes sabotage, I wrote an angry e-mail to her that she quickly copied to my CEO. Had I pursued any legal action against the agency, the e-mail would certainly have been used against me. As a word of caution, keep a lid on your emotions. Get your anger out through appropriate channels. Kick a box in the backyard, exercise, watch your favorite Godfather movie, do strenuous yardwork, or get involved in a project that addresses a favorite cause; but don't allow yourself to be provoked into a verbal or written battle with your bullies.

Leaving Your Job

After soul-searching and weighing the pros and cons, you've reached the conclusion that you've been in a love-hate relationship too long. You've loved, and your bullies have hated. It's time to go, in spite of the avenues you've pursued. Or, you've done some soul-searching and concluded that you no longer want to work in an abusive environment. You recognize that there are some things that cannot be changed.

Any careful person tries to line up another job before quitting. So if you're able, pull your résumé together and get it out there before resigning your post. You could also decide, if you've saved a little money, that you want to take a break from work for a while. On the other hand, by leaving your job, an opening has been created for you to pursue a dream, going back to school or opening up your own business, for example.

How you leave your organization means a lot as you look for new work and put your experience to rest. More importantly, when you reflect back on your difficult experience, you will not regret that you left with grace and dignity, along with your integrity intact. If possible, leave a job on good terms; but better yet, leave on *your* terms. Whatever you do, don't let others control your departure narrative.

Most people would say that a passive exit is probably the best, but experts Namie and Namie don't share that view. They strongly suggest that you carefully plan your getaway, but not one that jeopardizes your ability to move on with your life by putting your tail between your legs so that you don't offend anyone, especially your bullies. They recommend reviewing the law regarding defamation of character. Defamation is misrepresentation that can include any act, suggestion, or reference that leads a listener to believe something untruthful or misleading about another person, including even gestures, facial expressions, or voice inflections. You will likely have recorded accounts of your bully defaming you to others.

In addition, if an employer volunteers to another employer the reasons for your discharge or quitting, the first employer is guilty of a crime. An employer is only allowed to disclose truthful reasons for a discharge or voluntary termination of the employee if specifically asked without prompting (Namie & Namie, 2009).

While it takes a bit of courage and expense, these experts also recommend hiring a pre-employment reference-checking service to call your ex-employer for references and report their feedback. If your employer defames you, share this with an attorney, who will use their comments in a letter to them letting them know they will be held liable for the mistreatment you received if they release to future employers any information prohibited by law.

Perception is very important. Communicate about your departure in a positive light. It will have a strong impact on how others see you. You don't want to get into a situation where you are asked to remove office items before your ascribed departure date. Nor do you want to leave your bullies with any ammunition that will follow you along the career trail. Keep things private.

In addition, Namie and Namie recommend letting prospective employers know there was a conflict at your former job, and that they may not receive positive feedback from your bullies. Let the prospective employer know how you expect to be discredited, while directing positive comments from others toward the conversation.

It may be possible to work out a severance package. For example, in exchange for your keeping mum about your bullying experience, you receive an early-departure package. This could include money, travel or moving expenses, job coaching, résumé-building, or job recommendations. Also, get a promise of and receive a recommendation letter before your last day, so you have it with you when you leave.

Have a plan to move forward with your life. The best antidote for a bullying experience is to engage your mind with a project or new job. Boredom is not a friend when one is recovering from an abusive relationship, because the mind tends to try and make sense of something that doesn't make sense at all. Become engaged with something meaningful, and expect that grieving is a natural part of getting over your experience. Take a moment each day to grieve; express sadness, anger, and depression, but get on with your life. Keep a journal. Trust that your former employers are not giving any thought to you. If you come to mind at all, it may be with relief.

During your recovery period, nurture yourself. There are many ways of allowing yourself to salve your wounds as you move forward. Peer support can be very helpful, and blogging online has been a wonderful way for people to vent (there are any number of blogging sites). Give yourself permission to be comforted by others who've gone through their own bullying experiences.

Life does go on, and your life will more than likely be better following your assault. One woman has already cast her future toward the academic world, while another man has taken charge of a new agency's quality-management department. Both of these folks have used their suffering wisely, with the conviction that bullying will not be part of their work life again.

You *will* be okay.

Somebody said that it couldn't be done,

But he with a chuckle replied

That "maybe it couldn't" but he would be one

Who wouldn't say so till he'd tried.

So he buckled right in with the trace of a grin

On his face. If he worried he hid it.

He started to sing as he tackled the thing

That couldn't be done, and he did it.

There are thousands to tell you it cannot be done.

There are thousands who prophesy failure;

There are thousands to point out to you one by one,

The dangers that wait to assail you.

But just buckle in with a bit of a grin,

Just take off your coat and go to it;

Just start in to sing as you tackle the thing

That "cannot be done," and you'll do it.

Edgar Guest, "It Couldn't Be Done" (1919, p. 37)

Points of Change
Part II—Repairing the Tear in
Social Service Structures

It *is* possible to identify and repair torn social structures that contribute to workplace bullying. This book has shared a litany of reasons why many social service systems and individuals resist change. Yet, there also exist leaders who have a vested interest in transforming these flawed systems, especially when long-term gain equals enlightened client care, as well as worker well-being.

Individuals attempting to transform a dysfunctional workplace must imbed new bully-free policies, in addition to dealing with worker grief due to past bullying violations. There is a tendency for veteran staff to project their institutional memories onto new administrators, who must help them work through their anger and frustration.

Administrators who inherit past wrongdoing from their predecessors must support social service workers to move beyond their distrust, by establishing trust early on in their initial introduction. Leaders know they're moving in the right direction when staff comes to terms with a new social norm. This can take time, depending on how organization board members support senior management, and on senior management's accountability.

Addressing Workplace Bullying

In tough economies, people generally stay put in their workplaces. This can seem truer for those working within the social service system because their organizations are often donor- and government-funded. Workplace bullying thrives in harsh economic environments. Yet, abuse is abuse. Not to sound overly dramatic, one could compare the environment to immigrant conditions at the turn of the twentieth century, when newly transported immigrants were desperate to feed and clothe their families. They were forced to accept ridiculous work conditions because they were stuck. While workers nowadays are not likely to be threatened by physically abusive employers, workplace bullying is another form of abuse, a psychological one, and still a major cause of worker unease.

Bullying workplaces are overgrown gardens that need taming. The fact remains that one in three adults has been bullied on the job, and three-fourths of the bullying occurs from the top down (Workplace Bullying Institute and Zogby International Polling Survey, 2007). We all pay a terrible price, including our clients. Fear-based social structures constrict the workforce.

Real-Life Trial and Error Drives Innovative Workplace Reform

Mentioned in previous chapters, vertically managed entities, psychological estrangement, disparate mission focus, funding issues, shifting policies, and flawed communication drive much of bullying practices in social services. And negative and patterned behaviors and attitudes function to keep bully behavior rolling. At the same time, organizational memory strives to keep things the same because "It's what we're used to."

It seems strange that anti-bullying policies in the social service workplace are still considered innovative practice rather than normal workplace policy. This sense of innovation makes instituting and enforcing anti-bullying measures a challenge for social service organizations, especially in an environment where inertia and crisis coexist.

Developing a strategic plan to combat workplace bullying should be considered innovative, meaning that leaders must approach their strategy willing to take risks. Change comes through trial and error.

Mentioned throughout this book, change normally occurs at the top, when senior-level management and board members introduce and support anti-bullying policies. A strategic plan to address workplace bullying will not work unless both entities are onboard. The board's job is to make sure that new policies are created and implemented. It is senior management's work to operationalize the initiative and maintain fidelity to the process, without having inertia set in or crisis taking everyone off-focus. This means that social service organizations will have to become systems of perpetual learning (Schein, 2010).

Addressing Workplace Bullying to Create a Safe Work Environment

Experts make the following recommendations when taking action to prevent workplace bullying:

- Require board and senior-management commitment to establishing a bully-free workplace. Change is not possible unless senior staff and agency board members clearly message and implement an anti-bullying initiative. Senior staff, per a job-performance category within their work evaluation, should be able to recognize and address the problem. Actually, all performance evaluations should include a section on "adherence to creating a safe and bully-free work environment."

- Develop an anti-bullying policy. This should be developed within the human resources department to reflect the particular social service agency's philosophy and mission, complaint procedures, assurances, confidentiality, progressive disciplinary action, and culture. Along these lines, systems that monitor, investigate, discipline, and follow up on workplace bullying should be established, reviewed, and approved by an employment attorney.

- Provide training on workplace bullying, as well as worker-conduct expectations. Just as sexual harassment is part of workplace orientation, workplace bullying should be included as well, and part of yearly training reviews. Training should include identifying and reporting workplace bullies, and assurances that there will be no agency retaliation should there be disclosures.

- Confront, intervene, and consistently monitor workplace bullies. This may cause worker push-back at first; especially when workplace bullies happen to be long-time employees functioning in a workplace where inertia has taken hold. They will probably provide excuses for their behaviors. People rarely thank innovators. They will likely accuse leaders of making them the "fall-guys" and examples. They may think they're being unfairly targeted because, again, "We've been following these procedures for years." They may also threaten to take themselves elsewhere.

- Just do it! There should be nothing holding social services organizations back from enacting anti-bullying policies. Allowing bullying to occur at work sends a very strong message that management is not engaged. At the very least, it demonstrates a forward-thinking approach to managing a social services workforce, while demonstrating best practice. Most importantly, it supports employees to feel psychologically safe.

It All Begins at the Top

Stated earlier, experts agree that nothing changes within organizations unless leaders make it happen. But, in the past, leadership training has been mostly absent in social work training. A public misperception continues that individuals with people skills naturally have management skills, but social services education has historically neglected management training. Unique leadership skill sets are required in order to transform impaired social service structures into learning cultures. An advertisement for a transformation leader might look something like this:

Bold Leadership Needed! Wanted: persons with the following skill sets to address social service workplace bullying—

- Must make positive assumptions about human nature (the Y-management style), and understand that individuals are naturally drawn to doing the best they can when given an opportunity.

- Must be customer- and coworker-friendly. The candidate must value everyone served through the organization, by promoting an environment respectful to clients and coworkers.

- Must sustain open communication and transparency within the organization, characterized by the ability to tolerate scrutiny. Transparency demonstrates that what leaders do does not include advancing their own agendas.

- Must value every worker's job, orientation, skills, and personality.

- Must recognize the complexity and interconnection between worker satisfaction and client satisfaction, and the power of external and internal workplace relationship-building.

- Must be the role model you wish to see within your organization.

- Must be trustworthy. Working at a job is like a marriage; people don't trust if they've been deceived.

- Must have the ability to take risks and not be afraid to speak up or rock the boat.

- Must be committed to providing a learning work culture through inquiry and flexibility. A sign of authentic positive character is inquiry, and flexibility ensures that people are not afraid to do their best work, in spite of their fear of making mistakes.

- Must treat staff the way they would like to be treated. Sharing appreciation and encouragement is "free fuel" and takes little effort.

- Must maintain a commitment to best practice by continuously reviewing the mission.

- Must believe that maintaining control *is* control, and walking steadily through times when everything "hits the fan" is essential.

- Must have the ability to forecast the future, and evaluate current social service practices.

- Must have the ability to admit and learn from mistakes.

- Must be the message bearer for truth, and capable of communicating bad news.

- Must hold people accountable for their attitudes and behaviors that are counter to our agency's stated mission.

Disney World, Leadership, and Social Services

Changing workplace bullying entails not only commitment, but practical execution as well. Once social service leaders have made the commitment to address workplace bullying, they need to consider embedding new organization principles into their systems of care. A bully-free workplace is better functioning when the right principles are implemented. These principles are universal, and can apply as much to corporations as to social services organizations.

Lee Cockerell, former executive vice president of operations for the Walt Disney World Resort, outlines ten essential leadership principles in his book *Creating Magic* (2008), which are still taught at the Disney Institute. Lee led over 40,000 "cast members" for over ten years. He states, "The job was never about me. It was always about the people." Lee's innovations created a more innovative and friendly Disney.

Earlier in Lee's long career he encountered plenty of workplace bullies, and believes it was partly because they represented many former military personnel following World War II and the Korean War who used an autocratic style and fear to motivate workers. Lee had an epiphany when he realized, through his own on-the-job mistakes, that "intimidation is not the best way to manage people." Lee currently does a lot of leadership work with our military and reports that they also have adjusted to a more inclusive team work approach, and it is working (first interview January 24, 2011; reviewed December 8, 2012).

According to experts, the autocratic, top-down leadership approach existing within vertically managed organizations doesn't work. While most social services organizations have adopted a hierarchical structure, workers thrive more in participatory environments. Lee contributes, "If you want your employees to deliver excellent service, you'd better provide them with excellent leadership. Successful workplaces, he states in his book, are "clear, well-defined, and purposeful." Lee achieved leadership excellence by spreading responsibility and authority throughout the organization, understanding that everyone—at all levels—can demonstrate leadership and make a difference.

A little background . . .

When Lee took the job at Disney World in 1993, he'd already been working as the vice president of resort operations at Disneyland Paris, and had studied leadership principles for years. Leaders were needed to manage the business and inspire employees to adapt to twenty-first-century demands. In his book, he describes that transforming Disney World's resort work culture was a bit bumpy at first, until workers experienced the results. When the leadership philosophy was not implemented as quickly as he had hoped, Lee wrote up his principles in an easy-to-read format. Those principles are known as the "Disney Great Leader Strategies."

Rolling out the strategies, based on what to expect from Disney World leaders, took eight weeks. Every manager reviewed them, along with all cast members. Lee believes they are effective at every level of every industry, including social services. Leadership and training go hand-in-hand when it comes to transforming a work culture. These strategies can be used to address and reform social services workplace bullying as well. Five of these principles are highlighted below.

Applying Lee's Transformative Principles to Social Services

Lee Cockerell's principles focus on creating a workplace where learning and respect take priority. Within a learning culture, there is little time to blame or punish because everyone is required to help create solutions to work problems, and to interactively and productively engage with coworkers at all levels.

1. Remember, Everyone Is Important

A healthy work environment is inclusive, a place where people at all levels are engaged and viewed as important contributors. Letting employees know they matter is a big part of the message.

Transferring the magic by making everyone important . . .

Social service workers can all participate in creating their own performance goals that pertain to keeping the workplace respectful and bully-free.

In addition, workers can be welcomed to the organization personally by their team members through some form of get-together. And leaders can extend their personal welcome through texting, e-mailing, or meeting new employees in person.

With the understanding that social services organizations are relationship-based businesses, supervisors, as part of their performance evaluation, can set their own goals to demonstrate staff appreciation throughout the year. They can be on the lookout to catch people doing something right, provide immediate feedback, express gratitude, and make workers feel safe.

Leaders can spend more time in the field, instead of regularly relying on someone else's report. They can directly answer tough questions from staff. And, they can consistently employ direct reports to check on worker satisfaction and morale.

Social service leaders can lay to rest institutional memory, when workers participate in their own transformation by actively taking a role in embedding mutual concern for coworkers and clients with senior management. One enlightened social service leader regularly meets with different frontline workers for lunch in order to obtain their input and share his appreciation.

2. Break the Mold

Social services organizations must challenge conventional practice and strive to incorporate evidence-based practice into their systems of care. Establishing bully-free workplaces is best practice, and one way to break the mold when innovating a social services organization.

Transferring the magic by breaking the mold . . .

Fewer senior staff can interfere when frontline workers deviate from antiquated practices, easing the way for enlightened innovation. One example comes to mind. Decades ago, infant–mental health professionals were out-of-the-box thinkers when they challenged the conventional belief that infants and toddlers weren't affected by parental bonding. They kept chiseling away at these conventional beliefs, until people began to pay attention to their message. As a result, infants and toddlers are now assessed as carefully as other young clients in the social service arena, and workers are inspired by doing this work.

In addition, social services staff working within the same function areas, such as counseling, can be cross-trained to step in when there is need for additional client support. And social services organizations can begin a yearly in-house symposium where staff presents their program innovations and outcome data, as well as be recognized for their ideas, ingenuity, and creativity.

Organizations could promote interagency staff training. For example, human resources might introduce their workplace anti-bullying policy, while counseling staff describe their use of eye movement desensitization therapy with adolescents. Workers will gain better understanding and respect for job roles.

3. Hire the Right People

In his book, Lee discusses identifying and placing people in the right jobs in order to create worker satisfaction as well as quality services. By placing the right people in the right jobs, much potential bullying can be prevented.

Transferring the magic by hiring the right people . . .

Social service organizations normally have written job descriptions with corresponding skill sets, but there is a problem when these job descriptions are not reviewed as often as they need to be. Regular review of job descriptions should occur to ensure best practice, as well as innovation around anti-bullying policies.

Social service organizations must also be mindful of not hiring the same type of personalities year after year. This practice can stunt organization innovation and inhibit moving beyond what has "always been done," or is most comfortable for the inner power circle. My previous organization's discomfort with individuals unlike themselves was obvious when senior staff members basically shared the same personality characteristics. Sameness creates inertia, and bullying.

Good leaders and managers know to hire individuals more talented and smarter than themselves. Hiring the best talent creates a dynamic workforce. This would naturally pose a threat to workplace bullies, who do their best work intimidating new workers. My first supervisor held to the practice of encouraging her staff to excel, and clients were better for it. Her invitation to us to grow beyond her own capabilities prioritized clients and put us at ease. Leaders have a unique opportunity to communicate this intention when they look for qualified and dedicated staff.

Social services organizations can place the same emphasis on talent as they do on résumés, directly referring incoming résumés to the appropriate departments, rather than having them first screened by human resources staff. Human resources résumé screeners are not truly familiar with skill sets needed for every job, and often miss key indicators that reflect a candidate's qualifications. Because social services organizations are normally hierarchical, excellent candidates can be overlooked if they don't have precisely what human resources staff are looking for.

For example, a seasoned child care worker understands that a good candidate with a lesser academic degree may have more of a natural ability to work with children than another applicant with a higher degree. Unless a job requires someone with an advanced degree, job candidates, holding various diplomas, can be easily identified by veteran staff when they appropriately message their skills.

Asking candidates what captures their passions often reveals their commitment to social service work. Bully traits can be identified when a candidate is asked this question.

Social services agencies often make the mistake of hiring the first body that walks into a job interview, because some positions are difficult to fill. And persons with job qualifications may lack the appropriate temperament for the position. While it can cause temporary workplace stress, waiting to hire the most qualified candidate is the best way to go in the long run. It ultimately costs the organization less money, and disrupts client care less often.

4. Always Remember the Mission

It is an oxymoron to work in social services and be a bully. Bullies supply rationalizations about what it takes to get a job done, completely overlooking a very important part of the equation—their coworkers. Coworkers deserve the same consideration as clients.

Transferring the magic by always remembering the mission . . .

Regular review and discussion of agency mission can deter potential bullies from rationalizing their behaviors toward coworkers. Anti-bullying materials that include organization mission should be placed in key work locations, while customer service discussion should focus on treating everyone in the workplace with respect, in order to create the right environment to make an impact. In addition, any workplace newsletters can include regular articles relating the mission back to making the workplace a harmonious environment.

5. Training

Training on workplace bullying should be continuous, not a one-time thing. Healthy workplaces are continuously reviewing, learning, and growing.

Transferring the magic through training . . .

Leaders know that effective training includes surveying workers about their work experiences. In addition to other information, surveys provide feedback that helps facilitate educating and coaching bullies away from their negative behaviors.

Leaders also know that the workplace can be more effective when people are trained as a team. And camaraderie is established when successes are celebrated together.

Organization orientation should include teaching the principles of creating a healthy workplace. In addition, new staff should be taught that the organization's social structure has zero tolerance for bullying. It should also be communicated that reporting workplace bullying will be confidential, and without retaliation.

Because social service work is often driven by crisis, workers should learn during orientation how to accept the unexpected without losing their cool or undermining someone else's hard work.

Ongoing training should include how to effectively communicate with coworkers and clients, as well as problem-solve as a team. Workers should also be taught time-management, so that they don't bring additional stress to their work and allow it to spill over to client or coworker relationships.

Anti-bullying messaging and training takes place in the classroom, in the field, with supervisors, with coworkers, and through newsletters, learning-management systems, conferences, and symposiums. Even mistakes are important opportunities for personal and professional growth. Leaders set the tone for making learning part of system errors.

Transferring the magic to ourselves . . .

Far and away, the greatest teaching about on-the-job bullying comes from our own behavior, what we say and do, regardless of our position in the workplace. We make a difference. By recognizing, messaging, and role-modeling respectful workplace etiquette, we impact the next generation of social service providers.

When social services workplace bullying becomes recognized and addressed, a healthier and more enlightened workforce will emerge. There is much to gain.

> "One man with an idea in his head is in danger of being considered a madman, two with the same idea in common may be foolish, but can hardly be mad; ten men sharing an idea begin to act, a hundred draw attention as fanatics, a thousand and society begins to tremble, a hundred thousand and there is war abroad, and the cause has victories tangible and real; and why only a hundred thousand? Why not a hundred million and peace upon earth? You and I who agree together, it is we who have to answer that question."

William Morris, November 14, 1883

References

American Psychiatric Association. (1994). *Diagnostic and statistical manual of mental disorders* (4th ed.). Washington, DC: Author.

Beane, A. L. (2008). *Protect your child from bullying: Expert advice to help you recognize, prevent, and stop bullying before your child gets hurt.* San Francisco: Jossey-Bass.

Brohl, K. (2005). *The new miracle workers: Overcoming challenges in child welfare.* Washington, DC: CWLA Press.

Cockerell, L. (2008). *Creating magic: 10 common leadership strategies from a life at Disney.* New York: Random House.

Cohen, A. (2010). New laws target workplace bullying. *Time* magazine, July 21. Retrieved February 16, 2011, from http://www.time.com.

Conner, M. G. (2007, rev. 2009). Transference: Are you a biological time machine? *The Source*, winter, 2007. Retrieved January 4, 2008, from http://www.crisis counseling.com/Articles/Transference.htm.

Darley, J. M., & Latane, B. (1968). Bystander intervention in emergencies: Diffusion of responsibility. *Journal of Personality and Social Psychology, 8,* 377–383.

Davenport, N., Distler Schwartz, R., & Pursell Elliott, G. (2005). *Mobbing: Emotional abuse in the American workplace.* Collins, IA: Civil Society Publishing.

Fayol, H. (1916). Administration industrielle et generale. *Bulletin de la societé de l'industrie minérale.* (Henri Fayol was a French management theorist whose ideas about management and organization of labor were widely influential at the beginning of the twentieth century.)

Fisher-Blando, J. (2011). Workplace bullying: Aggressive behavior and its effect on job satisfaction and productivity (Doctoral dissertation, University of Phoenix, 2011).

Guest, E. A. (1919). *The path home.* Chicago: Reilly and Lee.

The Healthy Workplace Campaign. (2010). Healthy Workplace Bill. http://www.healthyworkplacebill.org.

Hemphill, P. (2011, November). *Treating sexual disorders in an outpatient setting.* Lecture presented at the annual conference of the Professional Recovery Network, Ponte Vedra, FL.

Johnson, F. (1976). Psychological alienation: Isolation and self-estrangement. *The Psychoanalytic Review, 3,* 369–402.

Kestin, S. (2011, April 3). Privatized child welfare brings top pay for execs. *Orlando Sentinel,* pp. 1–2.

Kiecolt-Glaser, J. K., & Glaser, R. (2010). Psychological stress, telomores and telomerase. http://www.ncbi.nlm.nih.gov/pmc/articles/PMC2856705/.

Leymann, H. (1990). Mobbing and psychological terror at workplaces. *Violence and Victims, 5*(2), 119–126.

Leymann, H., & Gustafsson, A. (1996). Mobbing at work and the development of post-traumatic stress disorders. *European Journal of Work and Organizational Psychology, 5*(2), 251–275.

Mandelker, D. (1956). Family responsibility under the American poor laws: I. *Michigan Law Review, 54,* 497–532.

McGregor, D. (1960). *The human side of enterprise.* New York: McGraw-Hill.

Namie, G., & Namie, R. (2009). *The bully at work.* Naperville, IL: Sourcebooks.

Namie, G., & Namie, R. (2011). *The bully free workplace.* Hoboken, NJ: John Wiley & Sons.

Omari, M. (2010, June 27). *The role of bystanders in workplace bullying.* No Workplace Bullies Web log post. Retrieved August 24, 2011, from http://nowork placebullies.blogspot.com/2010/06/role-of-bystanders-in-workplace.html.

Petrecca, L. (2010, December 28). Bullying in workplace is common, hard to fix. *USA Today,* front page.

Quigley, W. P. (1996). Five hundred years of English poor laws, 1349–1834: Regulating the working and nonworking poor. *Akron Law Review, 30,* 100–103.

Reamer, F. (1998). *Ethical standards in social work: A critical review of the NASW Code of Ethics.* Washington, DC: NASW Press.

Rumelt, R. P. (2011). *Good strategy–bad strategy: The difference and why it matters*. New York: Crown Business.

Schaefer, R. T., & Lamm, R. P. (2012). *Sociology*. New York: McGraw-Hill Publishing.

Schein, E. H. (2010). *Organizational culture and leadership, 4th edition*. Hoboken, NJ: Jossey-Bass.

Taylor, F. W. (1912). *Principles of scientific management*. Self-published.

U.S. Department of Health and Human Services. (2010). Bullying informational website. www.stopbullying.gov.

Workplace Bullying Institute. (2011). Frequently Asked Questions. http://www.workplacebullying.org/faq.php.

Workplace Bullying Institute and Zogby International Polling Survey (2007). *U.S. workplace bullying survey September, 2007*. Retrieved from http://workplacebullying.org/multi/pdf/WBIsurvey2007.pdf.

Yu, W. (2012, January/February). Workplace rudeness has a ripple effect. *Scientific American Mind*. Retrieved from http://www.scientificamerican.com.

Additional Resources

Babbel, S. (2011, May 22). Effects of trauma: Estrangement from family. *Psychology Today* [Psychology Today Web log post]. http://www.psychologytoday.com/blog/somatic-psychology/201107/effects-trauma-estrangement-family.

Baras, R. (2011, March 14). Bullying: How bystanders can stop workplace bullying [Family Matters Web log post]. http://www.ronitbaras.com/focus-on-the-family/parenting-family/bullying-20-how-bystanders-can-stop-workplace-bullying/#.UFPCr7Iia8A.

Boise State University School of Social Work. (n.d.). History of early social work. The Social Work History Station website: http://web1.boisestate.edu/socwork/dhuff/xx.htm.

Bolden, R., Gosling, J., Marturano, A., & Dennison, P. (2003). *A review of leadership theory and competency frameworks: Edited version of a report for Chase Consulting and the Management Standards Centre.* Center for leadership studies. Exeter, UK: University of Exeter. http://www2.fcsh.unl.pt/docentes/luisrodrigues/textos/Liderança.pdf.

Crowley, K., & Elster, K. (2009). *Working for you isn't working for me: The ultimate guide to managing your boss.* London: Penguin Books.

Crum, T. (1998). The shift toward private sector service delivery: Restructuring child welfare systems in the name of children. *Journal of Children and Poverty, 4*(2), 39–59.

Doyle, M. E., & Smith, M. K. (2001). Classical leadership. In the British online *Encyclopedia of informal education* (spring 2012). http://www.infed.org/leadership/traditional_leadership.htm.

Droege, S. B. (2006). Theory x and theory y. In *Encyclopedia of Management* (5th ed.). Farmington Hills, MI: Thomson Gale. Online access at http://www.enotes.com/management-encyclopedia/theory-x-theory-y.

Fischer, P., Krueger, J. I., Greitemeyer, T., Vogrincic, C., Kastenmüller, A., Frey, et al. (2011). The bystander-effect: A meta-analytic review on bystander intervention in dangerous and non-dangerous emergencies. *Psychological Bulletin, 137*(4), 517–537.

Hill, A. (2011, June 21). Don't let process hold back progress. *The Financial Times*, Business Life Section, p.10.

Hillman, J. (1999). *The force of character*. New York: Ballantine Publishing Group.

Internal Revenue Service. (2011). IRC-457(b) deferred compensation plans. http://www.irs.gov/Retirement-Plans/IRC-457(b)-Deferred-Compensation-Plans.

Kadushin, A. (1976). Child welfare services past and present. *Journal of Child Psychology,* winter ed., 51–55.

Kinosian, J. (2010). Workplace bullying: Do we need a law? *Parade* magazine, July 18. http://www.parade.com.

Lavagnino, J. (2009, May 11). Workplace bullying, harassment laws coming soon? *Law & Daily Life* [Web log post]. http://blogs.findlaw.com/law_and_life/2009/05/workplace-bullying-harassment-laws-coming-soon.html.

Office of the Inspector General. (2003). *The Tailhook report: The official inquiry into the events of Tailhook '91*. New York: St. Martin's Press.

Ouchi, W. G. (1981). *Theory z: How American business can meet the Japanese challenge*. Boston: Addison-Wesley.

Petr, C. G., & Spano, R. N. (1990). Evolution of social services for children with emotional disorders. *Social Work, 35*(3), 228–234.

Rachman, G. (2011, January 25). Where have all the thinkers gone? *The Financial Times,* Comment Section (p.11).

Repa, B. K. (2010). *Your rights in the workplace: An employee's guide to fair treatment, 9th ed.* Berkeley, CA: NOLO.

Tannenbaum, N., & Reisch, M. (2001, fall). From charitable volunteers to architects of social welfare: A brief history of social work. *Ongoing Magazine.* Access is available at http://ssw.umich.edu/ongoing/fall2001/briefhistory.html.

Weber, M. (1922). Wirtschaft und gesellschaft [Economy and society]. Trans. Hans H. Gerth (1951). (Max Weber was a German sociologist and engineer, recognized as a systems and management theorist.)

Weber, M. (English translation 1930). *The Protestant ethic and the spirit of capitalism*. Trans. Talcott Parsons. London: George Allen & Unwin Ltd. (For information on Weber, see Britannica Online, 2012, http://www.britannica.com/EBchecked/topic/638565/Max-Weber.)

Index

About the Author

Kathryn Brohl, LMFT, a licensed marriage and family therapist, has worked in social services for over thirty-five years. Author of six books that include two best-sellers, Ms. Brohl has lectured on trauma-informed care throughout the United States, Canada, and Australia. She has been an administrator, consultant, trainer, private practitioner, and frontline worker, and has been interviewed in national periodicals such as *USA Today*, *Parents Magazine*, and *Children's Voice*, as well as the *Washington Post*, *Miami Herald*, and *Florida Times Union*. Ms. Brohl has written and implemented several start-up programs during her career, including a large child-welfare system and intensive outpatient and mental health programs.